Bumbling Humans

Reflections on Liberatory Change

Lucinda J. Garthwaite

ONION
RIVER

PRESS

Burlington, Vermont

Onion River Press
24 Maple Street, Suite 214
Burlington, VT 05401
www.onionriverpress.com

ISBN Paperback: 978-1-95718-442-5

ISBN eBook: 978-1-95718-443-2

Library of Congress Control Number: 2023918642

Contents

INTRODUCTION

Several years ago, I showed up at a friend's house a little too early in the morning without calling first. She lives quite a way up in the hills near my home, and only when I reached the bottom of the dirt road that ends at her driveway did the spring morning fog start to clear. Her house is old and simple, but her view is extravagant, tumbling down to the river, up over layers of woods and farms to a graceful wave of rounded hilltops. When I stepped out of my car in my friend's dooryard that day, the view was divided; the valley shrouded, the hilltops bathed in light.

My friend is much older than I am, and was surprised and barely awake when she opened the door to my knock. But she opened her arms when I said why I was there. I'd just learned of the death of a treasured friend. We'd known he was ill, but hadn't expected his passing. After we'd talked a while about his struggles, the way he died, and the many complexities leading up to his death, she grew quiet.

"Oh, my dear" she finally said, looking out at the hills, "We're all just bumbling humans."

She said it with love, and she said it with sadness, and I feel the same. We make mistakes and bad decisions. That's a part of the human condition. We're vulnerable to fear and to greed, and we struggle with difference, yet we never run out of ways to be human. Humans can think and reason, and even that fabulous gift creates havoc when we come to conclusions that make no sense, then set up senseless systems.

It's not always terrible. In fact, I'm inclined to believe that most

1

missteps, mistakes, and misguided decisions are just that. From those, often, with thoughtful practice and action, people and the planet can recover.

I think my friend is right, though. We bumble. We always have and, at least as far as my mind can imagine, we always will. So the work of creating a world where more people thrive in ever more peace will never be done.

Hang on, some object when they hear me say that. Can't we hope for liberation? Isn't that what we're working for?

To which I respond, absolutely. And sometimes. And not only.

Singular liberations have defined endings and beginnings. A person, group, community, or country is freed from something, like imprisonment, enslavement, or a repressive regime. Or they are freed to something; they can now vote. They can now marry. They can now move freely through a city in a wheelchair.

These are things to organize, protest, lobby, vote and legislate for and against, absolutely. And humans are vulnerable to greed and fear and errors in thinking, so some singular liberations last, or they sweep back around and need liberating again.

In a 1965 speech in Montgomery, Alabama, Dr. Martin Luther King first spoke the now famous words, "How long? Not long, because the arc of the moral universe is long, but it bends toward justice."

King reached back for that notion to a sermon over a hundred years earlier, in 1863, in which the abolitionist, Unitarian minister Theodore Parker said, "I do not pretend to understand the moral universe. The arc is a long one. My eye reaches but little ways. I cannot calculate the curve and complete the figure by experience of sight. I can divine it by conscience. And from what I see I am sure it bends toward justice."

Parker was preaching an activist faith. King was answering a question he knew was on the minds of his listeners, "Somebody's asking," he said,

'How long will prejudice blind the visions of men, darken

their understanding, and drive bright-eyed wisdom from her sacred throne?' Somebody's asking, 'When will wounded justice, lying prostrate on the streets of Selma and Birmingham and communities all over the South, be lifted from this dust of shame to reign supreme?'"

To which he replied, "Not long."

But here we are. I write this almost 70 years since Dr. King promised it wouldn't be long until prejudice would be vanquished, and justice would prevail. And I need not look far for proof that's not yet so.

Have things gotten better since 1965? Certainly. Have some things gotten worse? Also, depending on one's perspective, certainly. Is there still work to be done for singular liberations? Absolutely. But if I rest my hope only on singular liberation, I leave myself open to debilitating despair. Because we bumble. And because the only thing truly certain is change.

Despair is not the only risk of focusing solely on singular liberation. As big a risk, or bigger, is missing the chance to act every single day for liberatory change. Neither Theodore Parker nor Dr. King said the arc of the moral universe reaches justice. They said it bends in that direction. Parker was clear that he couldn't see the end of it. Both men put their faith in change.

Change never stops changing. That's true of every system on the planet. It's true of trees and forests and waterways. It's true of cities and towns. Buildings crumble, people move in, and they move away. Individual people never stop changing, nor do relationships, or networks of relationships as small as families and as large as the largest nation.

But change as a word is neutral, and I'm not interested in just any kind of change. I'm interested in liberatory change, change characterized by ever-increasing numbers of people freed from violence, and ever-increasing numbers of people free to thrive as who they are and who they are becoming.

And here's good news, the character of change in any system is affected by the behavior of its parts. In human systems like organizations, communities, states, and nations, the most pertinent parts are people. I am a person. My behavior can affect the character of change in the systems of which I am a part, and those changed systems can generate larger change.

So I want to understand how to behave. I have lived long enough to have messed that up plenty. With both good and questionable intentions, I have caused harm to others. I have contributed to organizational and social systems that have made it harder for some people and the planet to thrive. That whole time, I was advocating and voting and otherwise working for singular liberations. I was missing the work of liberatory change.

I'd like to change that. I'd like my daily behavior to align with change defined by more people thriving in ever more peace. I understand that is a practice, and as you'll read again in these pages, practice actually never makes perfect; it only makes change. So, I can only commit to a practice that aligns ever more closely with liberatory change. Forever–as long as I live. Like liberatory change itself, I'll never be done.

I want to be clear; I feel fierce about this. As much as I know that change is the only thing, we need to step up the pace. By we, I mean me, and anyone else who cares about bending the long arc of the moral universe ever toward justice. As I wrote this introduction, no doubt, more injustice was done, more lives were lost. The breath of the climate thinned. The planet groaned.

It's long past time to do things differently.

The reflections in this book are about that. I'm thinking as I write—about how I can behave differently in my daily life. About how to do things differently. These small essays started as part of the newsletter of the Institute for Liberatory Innovation, in which I'm privileged to think aloud twice a month with subscribers. Now I'm privileged to think aloud with you.

Thank you, in advance, for that.

CHOOSING STONES

For many who I know, read, and listen to, these past few years especially have been a time of critical transition, an opportunity to reckon and change in ways long overdue. With that awareness comes a hunger for information and understanding. It's an urgent hunger, with often anxious questions, because the stakes are so high. What do I need to know right now? If I miss a development on some critical action front, am I not paying enough attention? Is my privilege/bias/prejudice/discomfort keeping me from seeing what I need to see?

In conversations with friends and colleagues I've begun to see that this anxious urge to gather a perfect collection of understanding distracts me from the whole point of learning, which is to be changed—and to apply my changing self in the service of ever more equity, justice, kindness, and peace.

Three stories came to mind this week to remind me of this.

I visited the Grand Canyon only once, long enough ago that my camera was full of film. I remember that I felt a sort of panic there, which I soothed only a little by taking picture after picture of the canyon. I think I went through three rolls of film. I knew I was standing on the edge of Awesome. I thought I needed to take that with me, so, I took what I could with the camera. I have none of those photographs left today. I have no details to report to you, only, vaguely, that there were stripes and colors on the canyon walls.

Almost thirty years later, though, I remember well the feeling I had just before that panic set in. That feeling has stopped me in my tracks many, many times. I call them Grand Canyon Moments. What I took away was not the canyon, but a capacity to recognize the profound and the glorious, not only in natural wonders but in stories and poems, in people, in thinking, in gestures of care. That capacity is what allows me to hold on to hope, that essential fuel for change.

Another story: Some years ago, I was introduced to someone whose work I had admired for a long time already. So I was not surprised to hear, but nevertheless transfixed by, her startling clarity of thought and moral integrity, especially about human vulnerabilities, and how that affects social change. We live far apart and seldom see each other, but we talk often on the phone. I used to write frantically during those conversations, compelled by the fundamental importance of what she was saying, worried I would forget.

Eventually we settled into friendship, and I no longer take notes while we talk. I write things down occasionally, but mostly I pay attention. I listen, I ask questions, I respond to hers. So now I also know that my friend is wickedly funny (I'm smiling as I type.) I know some of her own vulnerabilities and worries, delights and losses, small senses of pride. I experience much more deeply her humanity, as she experiences mine. Our relationship — what neither of us could make alone — moves me as much as her moral clarity. I've never stopped being stunned by her insight, but it's our relationship that encourages me without end to lean ever harder into the work of change. If I had focused only on recording her remarkable insight, I would have missed the gift of our friendship.

One last story: There's a beach where I love to walk; it's just before what's called the Race, a constant roil of water where Cape Cod Bay meets the Atlantic. A few hours before and after low tide, that beach is covered with the smoothest of stones. I can't get enough of them. Really, literally, I cannot get enough of those stones. I walk that beach looking down, then bending to snatch a perfect White oval, the grey ones with a single line of White, the stones I can see the light through. I leave the beach with my pockets full, but for every stone I keep there are thousands I've left behind. I've also unchosen a few, tossing them back into the bay. Every time I do that, as the stone leaves my hand, I feel a moment of worry; should I have kept it?

In the end I have the stones I have. They are the ones I could take in, those I chose as carefully as I could. Some I have given away. The rest are in a bowl on a shelf behind where I sit to write. I used to look constantly for another bowl, a bigger one or a different shape, but lately I've been content with the bowl I've got.

The life I choose includes putting my hands alongside and after countless others, endlessly bending the arc of history toward liberation. In that effort there will always be insights I miss or leave behind. I can be sure I will not see all there is to see, or learn all I need to learn.

What's important, though, is staying open to being changed by what I do see, and by the bigger lessons around the details. It's risking missteps and failures that will come from what I neglect and ignore. It's choosing, over and over again, to keep my hands to the effort, accepting imperfection as part of the work.

Good Reasons for New Questions

Early in 2022, I read an interesting story about suitcases. Swedish journalist Katrine Marçalv begins the story by writing that in 1970 a U.S. luggage company executive, "unscrewed four castors from a wardrobe and fixed them to a suitcase... put a strap on his contraption and trotted it gleefully around his house," thus inventing the wheelie.

Except, as Marçalv quickly points out, that's not quite true, not, at least, the inventing part.

As she researched a book about women and innovation, Marçalv came across a 1952 photograph of a woman with a wheeled suitcase, and other evidence of suitcases on wheels as far back as the 1940s. But the luggage industry didn't embrace the wheelie until the early 1970s. Why?

Marçalv discovered the answer: gender roles and stereotypes. Men, the reasoning went, did not need wheels; they could carry their suitcases. Women didn't need them because they traveled with men, who carried their suitcases, too.

Assumptions about gender quashed suitcase innovation for decades, until the industry finally acknowledged that women did travel alone. Then the industry took credit for the wheelie and marketed it to women. Not until a male airline pilot created the cabin bag in 1987 did men become part of the market. Now wheeled luggage is virtually all there is.[1]

Here's another story, more recent and more serious. As the Covid pandemic overtook the world, two researchers in Texas developed a Covid-19 vaccine, called Corbevax, which was remarkably easy and cheap to make, using a decades-old approach that had proven effective not only for the Covid-19 virus but for earlier SARs varieties, and hepatitis as well. So why didn't more of us hear about it? According to the researchers who developed Corbevax, Peter Hotez and Maria Elena Bottazzi, it's because they "couldn't get any traction in the U.S. [government]... People were so fixated on innovation that nobody thought, 'Hey, maybe we could use a low-cost, durable, easy-breezy vaccine that can vaccinate the whole world.'"

Private philanthropists eventually funded the researchers' work, and unlike pharmaceutical companies, Hotez and Bottazzi gave the vaccine recipe away for free, mostly in countries outside the U.S. Writing about this story for NPR news, journalist Joe Palca makes the case that the US government's over-zealousness for innovation slowed the progress of innovation. It's worth asking also, I think, if the lack of opportunity for profit slowed that progress too.[2]

Another story, this one told by Yale Psychologist Phillip Atifa Goff and journalist Shankar Vedantam:

In 2003, fifteen-year-old Denver, Colorado resident Paul Childs, who struggled with mental illness, became seriously agitated at his family's home and brandished a kitchen knife. His family called 911. Police arrived, and as the situation escalated, shot and killed Paul Childs. At a subsequent press conference, Denver Police Department Division Chief Tracee Keesee, who is Black, was asked by a woman in the audience, "Does your police department train your officers to kill young Black men?" Goff describes Keesee's pause before she responded, "I don't know."

Keesee and Goff eventually began to collaborate in an effort to answer that question. Goff affirms that data solidly evidences a far larger percentage of Black Americans accosted and killed by police than white Americans. In response to Vedantam asking if Goff shares that experience, Goff replies, "I'm a Black man in America; of course I have. If you're Black in the United States and this hasn't happened to you, you're living a vanishingly rare life."

But Goff and Vendantum make the case that the problem of police violence against people of color has been wrongly defined in public discourse. Goff reminds us that there are more than 18,000 law enforcement agencies in the country, plus everyone who can call 911, and can, says Goff, "use law enforcement as their personal racism concierge." He continues, "If the problem is individual character, inside hearts and minds, a defect of the soul, ... then we're dealing with a problem that can't be fixed."

So Goff and Keesee went after different ways in, asking different questions, for example: In what specific situations do most incidents of police shootings of Black men occur? One answer was when police chase people on foot. Based on that information, and information about the physical and emotional state of almost all officers during foot chases, the researchers asked another question: What if officers took a deep breath before they started to run? The answer: When police were supported to take that deep breath, incidents of Black deaths at the hands of police decreased by twenty-three percent.[3]

One deep breath.

One deep breath is all it took for twenty-three percent fewer human beings to lose their lives.

The story of the wheelie suitcase is largely one of commercial gain and convenience, stymied by bigoted assumptions about gender. That's illustrative of a widely accepted understanding that gender assumptions limit us in myriad ways.

The story of the vaccine? That slowing of innovation probably contributed to serious illness and death among millions of people, many of them—and this is deeply noteworthy—Black and brown-skinned.

The story about police taking deep breaths before foot chases, of those deep breaths reducing by almost a quarter Black death at the end of those chases? That's as good a reason to ask new questions as I have ever heard.

Phillip Atifa Goff describes a "kind of neglect, a negligence in the way we ask questions," about police violence. That negligence impedes countless innovations in the service of a less violent future.

It's a life and death negligence, urgently demanding a sharpened collective ability see things differently. It's a very good reason to ask new questions.

The Danger of Naming Them Evil

In the spring of 2020, when many beyond his community finally learned that Ahmaud Arbery, a Black man, a 25-year-old aspiring electrician and fitness buff on a morning run, had been chased down and shot dead in February by a white father and son, his killers, Gregory and Travis McMichael, were quickly labeled evil—singularly, aberrantly, essentially so.

So was Derek Chauvin, the police officer who knelt on the neck of George Floyd while a growing circle of people protested and called for the officer to let Floyd breathe while three other officers stood by, watching. Floyd, by all accounts a "gentle giant" who'd led a gospel choir and was a great dad to his son and daughter, died before the ambulance arrived. The video of him begging for his life and calling for his mother is incontrovertible evidence of brutality.

That these murders were heinous acts of violent racism is not in question here. Of course, those deaths were singularly devastating, to their loved ones and to Black people especially. And if we focus our outrage on the evil or actions of specific people, we risk missing what public philosopher Elizabeth Minnich calls *extensive* evil, that is, "massive, monstrous harms carried out by many, many people over significant periods of time."[4] Arbery's and Floyd's murders were two among hundreds and hundreds of years of racist violence at the hands of white people, the foundation of which is baked into social structures and cultures all over the world.

Minnich warns against conflating that kind of evil with what she calls *intensive* evils, the acts of one or a few. Focusing here distracts us, she argues, from extensive evils. It becomes too easy to focus on the singular actor, to focus on punishment for the Derek Chauvins, the Gregory and Travis McMichaels, then once that punishment is accomplished, to turn away from the extensive evil of which their actions are a part.

When the video of Floyd's murder spread around the world, much of the world erupted in protest. But I am not confident that eruption uniformly recognized extensive evil. Why, if it did, did such protest, especially among white people, not erupt decades sooner?

Ignoring extensive evil is one danger of calling individual actors evil, of defining their entire character with that one word. That danger was evidenced for me on the day the world learned that the McMichaels had been arrested and charged for Ahmaud Arbery's murder. Social media exploded that day with certainty that these two men were nothing but evil, and by midafternoon the counter-argument had begun in the form of a new, private Facebook page called "Justice for Gregory and Travis McMichael."

I couldn't access the private page, but a screenshot that made it to my feeds included an affectionate photo of father and son, and this description, "These 2 God fearing men were only trying to protect their neighborhood. The area has had a string of break-ins and this man fit the description and did not comply with simple commands. Our hearts go out to the McMichael family in their time of need. Amen." At the time the screenshot was taken, the page had 18,487 members.

There is so much wrong here; Ahmaud Arbery only "fit the description" of being Black, and show me one white man who would "comply with simple commands" by two Black strangers. But that's for another conversation.

That such a page would emerge was, to my mind, inevitable. Here's why: without exception, people are complex creatures. No one can be fully defined by one aspect of their character, behavior, culture, or appearance. Still, it's a paradox of human thinking that it's easy to limit the complexity of people perceived as different, and absolutely un-abideable when it happens to people perceived as aligned with shared community, values, or identity.

I believe, in fact, that it feels like violence, or at least the threat of violence, because violence begins with—is made possible by—characterizing another human being as less than fully human, as essentially one thing.

Of course there were 18,487 people liking that page that first morning (and, I am certain, eventually many more) who thought of themselves as god-fearing, protective of their communities and families, who would feel vulnerable if their neighborhood experienced a string of break-ins. I imagine they either don't accept the concept of systemic racism, live in denial of the racism of their peers, or fully buy into a racist perspective. In any case, they see these men characterized as less than fully human, as only one thing, evil, and of course they respond defensively. Then they go on the offense because, as they've made clear, they identify as protective of their own.

So, what did it accomplish, identifying the McMichaels as nothing but evil, as unworthy of their complex humanity? Within hours of the appearance of the "Justice for Gregory and Travis McMichael" page, another page, "Actual Justice for Gregory and Travis McMichael" appeared with the simple description, "Let's pray these good ol' boys get the justice they so richly deserve." The picture at the top of the page is of a historical guillotine.

Arguably, that name-calling and invocation of violence distracted from the all-encompassing racism that makes those killings possible, and it may have exacerbated escalations of violence, because people cannot abide by reductions of whole human beings, to whom they relate, to one thing.

I'm not making an argument against accountability, or against outcry both organized and not. I'm absolutely not for diminishing the unbearable loss of life and love, the irretrievable trauma of people of color that's sharpened by each new death. I'm suggesting that the knee-jerk response of naming a person who commits a racist murder as singularly evil will do nothing to undermine—and arguably feeds — racism. In the work of creating a world in which racism erodes with each passing day, I believe in the need to be focused, disciplined, and strategic. Distracting from extensive evil and inviting violence is simply strategically unsound.

BREAKING THE RHYTHM

The poet and novelist Robert Penn Warren was born at the start of the twentieth century and died toward its end. He is known as much for his writing as for his loving criticism of the American South. After the 1954 U.S. Supreme Court Brown vs. Board of Education decision deeming segregation by race unconstitutional, Warren traveled the south to ask Southerners of all stripes what they thought of that decision. In the book he published of those conversations, Warren wrote, "In a country where moral identity is hard to come by, the South, because it has had to deal concretely with [this] moral problem, may offer some leadership. And we need any we can get if we are to break out of the national rhythm, the rhythm between complacency and panic."[5]

I read Warren's words as the world erupted in response to George Floyd's murder, among others. In my mind I replaced Warren's words, "the South" with "white people." White folks, myself included, having abetted, benefitted from and in many cases intentionally created structural racism for hundreds of years, indeed have to deal with a very complex moral problem. Arguably, many white folks took up this moral cause for the first time, or more assertively, in the wake of Floyd's murder. For some that was cause for hope.

But the phrase in the Warren quote that got me sitting up and paying new attention is this: "the national rhythm, the rhythm between complacency and panic." That hits me as an apt description—deeply, disturbingly true, and it has me worried. White concern about racism seems to have quieted again as I write from the distance of a couple years later. It's possible that it has settled into regular, necessary routines, systemized responses rather than protests in streets. It's also possible that what I saw in those weeks following Floyd's murder was panic, and panic is not known for clear thinking or staying power.

Change rooted in panic can be fickle, easily undone or affirmed by the ebbs and flows of political process.

Resistance to the changes called for in those weeks was and is fierce, on the street, on social media, in school board meetings, in the highest levels of state and national leadership. If any of that protest by white folks was simply a panic brought on by a killing that was finally unspeakable enough for white people who had remained on the sidelines before, will it stand up to a well-organized, determined, and powerful resistance?

Or will the mass of people, overwhelmingly white, who found themselves finally disturbed enough to act, swing back to complacency? Have they already?

Despite his criticism of racism in the South, Warren was writing at a time when "nation" too often implied "white." So, it's worth asking: is this indeed the tendency of many white folks, to panic when something public and heinous and racist happens, then rest in complacency later on? If that is even remotely possibly so (and I think it is), it seems to me worth recognizing complacency, and panic, neither of which will lead to sustainable change.

What *will* lead to change is persistent attention to whatever systems a person can do something about, understanding the work is never done. For that I call not so much on patience as steadiness, holding my rage and grief without being derailed by panic. I practice the discipline of seeing and listening and noticing when I step back. If it's only to rest and soon step back in, it's alright, even necessary. If it's only to look away, to return to unworried complacency, then I'm back in that national rhythm of which Robert Penn Warren wrote, and I'd better get back to breaking it.

LIBERATING RELATIONSHIPS

In 2013, writer and activist adrienne maree brown mused in a blog post about the possibility that the world may have entered what she called "a dark age." In such a time, she wondered if the legacy of people who work for liberation would be that they "maintained and remembered the way to love... [including] vulnerability, attachment, care, attunement."

Love, brown concluded, is a radical strategy.[6]

I don't know if we're in a dark age, but it does seem to me there's a shift in the air, both promising and terrifying. The question of what to do in the midst of this turning looms large. Traditional activism —organizing, advocating, taking to the streets—is not always accessible or possible for all kinds of good reasons.

Minding my own behavior with others, though, is always possible, and some of the best work I can do in the service of liberatory change is in my relationships.

It's not hard to find research and strong thinking in support of this belief. Scholar and teacher Linda Potter Crumley argues that "communication is both the cradle and the crucible of social justice," and relationships are where "social justice is constituted and sustained[7]." Buddhist teacher Kate Johnson writes, "Through wise relationships, it is possible to transform the barriers created by societal injustice."[8]

brown suggests that what she calls *liberated relationships* "are one of the ways we actually create abundant justice, the understanding that there is enough attention, care, resource, and connection for all of us to access belonging, to be in our dignity, and to be safe in community."[9]

That's powerful medicine right there, but it does not always go down easily. In my experience, these kinds of relationships are never consistently easy. With grateful respect to adrienne maree brown, I think of these relationships as liberat*ing*, rather than liberat*ed*, because they are constantly pushing against a long, long history of limitation. When I am in relationship with friends, family, and colleagues whose experience of the world is strikingly different than mine, I have to keep paddling against that wind. Liberating relationships require my loving, alert attention all the time.

Social psychologist Kiara Sanchez and her colleagues suggest that part of the reason that kind of attention is necessary lies in what they call "threatening opportunities." In three separate studies, Sanchez and her colleagues found that both white and Black-identified people saw the life-and-society-changing opportunity in multi-racial relation-ships. They also saw risks, especially in disclosing their particular experiences of being white or Black in the world.

The key to balancing those risks was facing together what Sanchez and colleagues describe as "race related parts of each other." Without "acknowledge[ing] and try[ing] to understand" those aspects of one another's lives, they suggest, inter-racial friends risk failing at friendship in critical ways.[10]

In a keynote speech at the 2021 St. Louis Racial Equity Summit, brown speaks to the role of love in mitigating these risks when she says, "Consider what love does in the face of dishonesty, faith-lessness, and repression: love tells the truth."[11] Part of what it means to be in liberating relationships is to tell the truth. It's also critically important, especially for the person in the relationship who has benefitted from a particular history or current systems, to *hear* the truth, the often painful, uncomfortable truth.

In my experience it also means celebrating joyful realities, cultures, and customs when those are not available to me. Even my adult stepdaughter, with whom I've shared a household and great love since she was 8 years old, has beloved cultural touchstones associated with being a Black woman that are not for me. My response, in the interest of a liberating relationship with her, is not to feel left out, but to be simply and graciously glad for her. Grace is part of liberating relationships. Humility is as well. So is building the muscle to sit with deep grief. So is accountability, forgiveness, sometimes reparation, and always compassion.

In that keynote, brown continued, "Love invites us home, love says we belong, unconditionally. Love does not demand our perfection, because none of us have that." Liberatory relationships require accepting imperfections and mistakes, our own and each other's, eschewing guilt in favor of acknowledging harm and demonstrable commitment to change.

Like so much else about change making, liberating relationships require practice, returning again and again to the mutual endeavor of shaking off the distractions of guilt, despair, and the long history of all kinds of systems that seek to separate human beings—to return to love.

I know little for certain, but I know the feeling when my family, my friends, my colleagues and I are in that particular circle of light that is a liberating relationship. I know our effort with one another is more than a small thing. I know we are a part of an ever-emerging, abundant justice.

THE RISK OF ANSWERS

There's risk in some answers, though questions beg answers, of course—some quite straightforward. Consider the woodshed I built some years ago; is it leaning a little downhill? The straightforward answer is yes—no matter how you look at it, that woodshed is most definitely leaning.

The next question is whether to do anything about that. Not at all, one neighbor says, it's charming that way. Definitely, says another, you'll be lucky if you get through the winter.

And if I decide to do something, then what? Brace it? Rebuild? And if I rebuild, then what design will best mitigate the slope of the hill? And how big to build it; how much firewood will we need, how will our family change, how will the climate?

That straightforward answer got complex fast. And the question had only to do with a lopsided shed.

And the answers depended on subjective things, like what is the nature of charming? The promise of whatever answer I come up with is that we'll get a sturdier shelter for our winter's wood. The risk is that we'll lose some charm, or build in a way that won't actually beat the slope of the hill, and we'll have to do it all over again.

The same is true for answers to questions far more complex. Does systemic racism exist? I say yes. Does white supremacy? Again, I say yes. But how to define them? How to respond? Those answers might be as unsteady as my lopsided woodshed, which I will now confess I set not on a leveled foundation, but on big stones of various shapes, and those have shifted over time. Given what I knew about building, and what I didn't know about shifting ground or building on even the slightest of slopes, I thought those stones would do. I was wrong.

Too often in history people in power, no matter their politics, have demanded allegiance to answers built on ideas they believe in as much as I believed in those stones. They might be right, and their answers may deliver what they promise, but they are just as likely wrong, or they were right at the time but like the ground under my woodshed, things changed. Still, many have died simply for questioning somebody's idea of a solid stone.

Answers promise paths forward, solutions to problems. Still, answers can be risky. Educator and public philosopher Elizabeth Minnich would seem to agree. "In truth," she has said, "it is not answers in which I place trust, for which I hope: it is the spirit of troubling."[12] Troubling, I take to mean, is stirring things up, and the willingness to wade in the mess that results. Troubling requires humility, the discipline to say, this is just one possible answer; will you think with me about it?

Thinking together is a powerful way to mitigate the risk of answers. Dr. Minnich has also said, "The more we hear from each other as we're thinking, the richer, the less closed, the more complex, the more subtle, the more in touch with the world we share we'll be."

So back to my woodshed, what if instead of asking a dozen questions and seeking specific answers, I simply wonder aloud with a friend, or better, a few friends: What it would take to make that shed right again?

Specific questions tend to arise from particular perspectives, pre-determined beliefs that can limit thinking. If I come to the question of my shed seeking answers aligned with just my own thinking—my shed looks bad, I must have a good-looking shed, I must have a lot of wood for the coming winter—I'll find answers aligned with my thinking as well.

And I think that applies to the challenges of a lopsided world, as well. So I'll seek when I can to think with others to find ways forward, as Minnich suggests, that are richer, more complex, more subtle, more in touch with the whole of the world.

INSISTENT WITNESS

In a 2020 interview, Bryan Stevenson—activist, attorney, teacher, writer, and founder and executive director of the Equal Justice Initiative[13]—told a story his grandmother told him of his great-grandfather, a literate man who had been enslaved, standing to read the newspaper to other formerly enslaved people at his home each evening. His daughter remembered sitting next to him as he read each night, loving the feeling of power in his reading, the calm that settled in as people for whom the news of the day had been forbidden listened carefully and took it in.

In telling him that story, says Stevenson, his grandmother was demonstrating what he calls, "the long view... the power of an eternal witness." She had, like a lot of older Black people he knew, "an instinct for creating these memories that just shape you for the rest of your life."

Popular understanding of the term "witness" generally rests in legal proceedings, or proclaiming theology, or simply seeing something happen. Witnessing in these ways has to do with verifying truth. But the kind of witness Stevenson describes seems to be something different.

I am reminded of a 1993 poetry anthology edited by Carolyn Forché, *Against Forgetting: Twentieth Century Poetry of Witness*. It is a collection of poems of genocide, violent repression, and war. These are difficult poems to read, and when I first read them they called me into a more serious consideration of those histories and my responsibility in their long wake. In her introduction to the anthology, Forché suggests that these poems "call on us from the other side of extremity and cannot be judged by simple notions of 'accuracy' or 'truth to life.' " These poems, she says, "will have to be judged by their consequences."

And that reminds me of a classic essay by the writer and activist Audre Lorde, "Poetry is Not A Luxury," (1985)[14] which begins with this, "The quality of light by which we scrutinize our lives has direct bearing upon the product which we live, and upon the changes which we hope to bring about through those lives."

So it seems there is another kind of witness to consider, the kind of witness that works against forgetting, that requires us to scrutinize our lives for their impact in the world. This other kind of witness is defined by its staying power and its consequence. This kind of witness is weighted by strong imagery, so it shows up in stories and poems, in dance, music, and visual art.

Forché writes that the witness reflected in the poems she collected generate "insistent memory." She says that "makes the world habitable... makes life possible." Lorde speaks to a "direct bearing" on how we live, Stevenson to the "shaping of our lives."

That is mighty stuff. It calls on us to recognize this insistent witness, to take up the light it offers, to, as Lorde suggests, "scrutinize our lives." Because as small a thing as each life may seem, it is each life and the way it's lived that carries hope and the possibility of change.

PEACE WITHOUT PUNISHMENT

What if we lived in a world entirely without punishment? Peace without punishment is not at all a new idea; it has worked for millennia for many of the world's people. Indigenous people of what is now known as the United States and Canada managed for centuries to maintain peace within communities with practices centering accountability and reconnection. Since the mid-twentieth century, these practices have become more broadly applied and called alternative dispute resolution, restorative justice, or restorative practice. But before that, as one Mashpee-Wampanoag writer has said, it was simply, "some of the tribal people [doing] what they had always done."[15]

My friend and colleague Dr. Olufemi Pamela Kennebrew reminded me also of *Ubunto*, a philosophy traditional in many African cultures dating back thousands of years, which also includes restoring victims to wholeness and integration of offenders back into community as critical to social harmony.

Responding to harm without punishment is clearly not new, and it works. It works in criminal justice, schools, and efforts to stem violence and jail for young people.[16] But U.S. prisons are fuller than in all but four other countries, and the United States nowhere to be found on a list of the 20 safest countries the world?[17] Why in the face of those facts among others do so many continue to insist that punishment is our protector?

I wonder if attachment to the idea of punishment is too culturally entrenched, if, in the West especially, individualism builds a falsely safe separation from those seen as different, deemed somehow more worthy of punishment.

In his 1999 book, *No Future Without Forgiveness*, South African Archbishop Desmond Tutu wrote that the concept of Ubuntu in particular is "very difficult to render into Western language." Our very languages, those translators of culture, ideology, and the character of a people, leave little room to consider that punishment is anathema to peace, that accountability, deep apology, and reconnection offer paths to healing and change, to justice.

Despite the challenge, Rev. Tutu tries to explain Ubuntu to Western ears, "my humanity is caught up and inextricably bound up in yours," he writes, "We are caught up in a bundle of life." For many—I know it was for me—it is frightening to consider bundling together with those who have done great harm, and difficult to accept that connection offers a clearer path to liberatory change than separation through punishment.

But punishment is not working. It is not keeping Black and brown people safe from police shootings. It is not keeping first responders safe from violence. It is not supporting loving families, housing, and food for children. It is not keeping disabled and trans people safe from beatings and worse. It has not made the lives of victims of violence more whole.

A teaching colleague of mine used to remind us often to "interrogate the dominant paradigm," by which she meant to critically question stubbornly unquestionable ideas and beliefs. The paradigm of punishment as a response to harm is certainly dominant; it's practically irrefutable in many circles, buoyed, no doubt, by fear. The stubborn refusal to be questioned, along with its very questionable results, is exactly what makes me question punishment as a path to less violence, and more peace.

CHECKING ASSUMPTIONS

Within the first few minutes of his inaugural address in January 2021, U.S. President Joseph Biden brought up national unity. To overcome our challenges, he said, would require, "Unity. Unity." That's not a typo; he said *unity* twice. Then, by my count, he said it 7 more times. "Without unity," he said, "there is no peace, only bitterness and fury."

Yikes, one would be justified in thinking, we'd better get some unity, and soon.

Or maybe not. Writer and journalist Tonya Russell pulls no punches when it comes to unity, "Please," she writes, "spare me your toxic positivity. Calls for 'unity and harmony' indicate that some want us to forgive and forget." After reminding us of overt threats not just to abstract freedoms but to the actual lives of Black, Indigenous, and other people of color; GLBTQ people; and people with disabilities, Russell continues, "remember, this isn't [just] a fight on the playground."[18]

Russell echoes the novelist Robert Jones, who wrote, "We can disagree and still love each other unless your disagreement is rooted in my oppression and denial of my humanity and right to exist." Jones is not having unity with people who wish him diminished, or worse, dead. A lot of other people are not having it either; if you search for that line, you'll find that it has become a most ubiquitous meme (by the way very often misattributed to James Baldwin; Jones posts on social media as "Son of Baldwin").

Harvard law professor Martha Minnow offers a slightly different critique, suggesting that unity too often comes with a requirement that, "groups that have been disadvantaged structurally [and] historically are often expected to be forgiving. Certainly, that's true for African Americans and women." In the same article, Yale historian David Blight warns of the lesson of unity "without justice" offered by the Civil War, which resulted in a *united* nation that nonetheless continued and encouraged violent systemic racism and white supremacy.[19]

Calls for unity often come along with calls for healing. That also sounds good, but restorative justice advocates warn that healing only happens in the wake of accountability, which is also a critical precursor to forgiveness. Admonitions from leaders to unify and heal too often leave that out. Still, when the harmed resist calls for unity, recriminations often begin. Tonya Russell feels this so strongly she was moved to exclaim, "We aren't monsters." Not being so sure about unity, "doesn't mean that we'll cause chaos or spread hate."

My point here isn't to take the wind completely out of the arguably hopeful sail of unity. Universal meaning is the thing I'm most concerned about, not unity itself. Universal meaning isn't real, not for the big concepts and ideas, and especially not in the United States, a country that writer and MSNBC news analyst Anand Giridharadas describes as, "… trying to do something that does not work in theory. To be a country of all the world, a country made up of all the countries, a country without a center of identity, without a default idea of what a human being is or looks like, without a shared religious belief, without a shared language that is people's first language at home".

That's a compelling description of what many have called the American Experiment. Giridharadas continues, "What we're trying to do is awesome. It is literally awesome in the correct sense of that word."[20]

And it won't work without slowing down to check out our assumptions that imbue concepts like unity with the same meaning or character. Ironically, those kinds of assumptions only separate, not, if you like, unify. Once I start checking these assumptions, things can get very interesting, and I've found that my world gets bigger, that I feel more connected because I understand better how others make meaning of their world.

The notion of chaos actually offers another example of an assumption. Tonya Russell relates chaos to hate and monsters. President Biden, continuing his description of life without unity, warned of a nation beset by, "no progress, only exhausting outrage, no nation, only a state of chaos."

So chaos is bad. But maybe not; Giridharadas continues, "It's scary out there right now. It's going to be scary for some time to come. What has been unleashed, what has been revealed, is ugly." But, he says, "If I lift my head to the horizon, I see a different picture. This is not the chaos of the beginning of something. This is the chaos of the end of something. . . .. We are living through a revolt against the future. The future will prevail."

That's an understanding of chaos I can embrace. It's hopeful, and I'm grateful to Giridharadas for inviting me to look at chaos from a different angle. This understanding of chaos invites me to imagine and to connect with others as we move into a more just and nonviolent future.

Without a healthy wariness of assumptions of meaning—a habit of thinking, *but wait, is there another way to see this?* I would have missed that hopeful reframe of chaos. I might have trumpeted unity to the detriment of my capacity to contribute to accountability and genuine healing. I don't want to miss those opportunities.

HOPE IS A STRATEGY

Just six weeks into 2021, an internet search for "hope" and "2021" yielded almost 2 million hits. "Don't lose hope" got half a million. Apparently, hope makes us happier. It makes us healthier. It motivates learning. It's good for business, though it is not, apparently, good for sales.[21]

In the interest of social change, though, hope has its detractors, among them the writer and activist Roxanne Gay, who writes, "I don't traffic in hope. Realism is more my ministry than is unbridled optimism." Gay continues, "When we hope, we abdicate responsibility. We allow ourselves to be complacent."[22]

The Czechoslovakian playwright, activist, and eventually president Václav Havel, distinguishing between hope and optimism, wrote, "Hope is definitely not the same as optimism. It is not the conviction that something will turn out well." Optimism, he wrote, is lazy. It seems to me that laziness is what Roxanne Gay is concerned about, but that unseeing insistence that things will get better is not even close to hope. With optimism set aside, the far greater heft of hope becomes clear.

Hope has far more gravitas than mere optimism. Hope is a necessary strategy in the slow work of carving out equity and driving down violence, precious enough in the work of change as to warrant our protection. Bryan Stevenson says hope is imperative. In fact, he is "persuaded that hopelessness is the enemy of justice." He continues, "You're either hopeful, or you're the problem. There's no neutral place." Hope, he often says, is a superpower.[23] That superpower, the steady efficacy of hope, has not gone unnoticed by those who value power more than justice. History is full of examples of hopelessness deployed to terrible effect.

All of this has made me aware of a solemn responsibility to safeguard hope. Not only throughout history but yesterday and just this morning, people chose hope in the face of headwinds far fiercer than any I have faced. I'm freshly suspicious of despair, including my own, when hope is the far more powerful way to stand in the wind.

Thinking as a Tool for Change

Thinking is often mistrusted as a path to change. This mistrust has come up in critiques of what some call a "Book Club Response" to racial injustice. Writer Tre Johnson spells it out, "When things get real—really murderous, really tragic, really violent or aggressive— my white, liberal, educated friends already know what to do. What they do is read. And talk about their reading. What they do is listen. And talk about how they listened." Johnson calls that a "slow road to meaningful change." All too often though, such thinking doesn't lead to change at all.[24]

Too often, thinking—particularly thinking aloud—becomes a camouflage for behaviors antithetical to change. Thinking can become performative, belying a lack of sincere commitment to step up or step aside in substantive ways. One arguably deadly example was the phenomenon of "jumping the line" for a Covid vaccine when they first became available, using connections and financial resources to access a vaccine ahead of people of color or with fewer financial resources. Some of those who got vaccines ahead of others in this way did so after having thought, perhaps even read, about the very structures that put those people at greater risk.

Such examples support the notion that thinking is never a path to change, but I believe it absolutely is; it's just limited, and vulnerable to misuse. What's generally considered activism—organizing, protesting, policymaking and the like—also has its limitations. Teacher and philosopher Elizabeth Minnich writes, "Acting against deep-rooted and massively prejudicial systems is no guarantee that we will liberate ourselves from, rather than just replace, them. They have the capacity to grow again if not ongoingly uprooted."[25]

Nothing can be uprooted unless we recognize the roots that need to go, and when it comes to "massively prejudicial systems," thinking is the tool for that job.

To be clear, thinking should not be confused with awareness. Awareness, one colleague pointed out to me, is a state—a noun. Rigorous, committed thinking is defined by learning, considering, self-reflecting, synthesizing, questioning, and discovering. Those are all verbs, what my elementary teachers told us were *action words*.

Serious activists engage in serious, even painful self-reflection as a critical precursor for change. Formal research, with the thinking that requires, has yielded insights that undergird and drive essential changes in policy, curriculum, and strategy. Collaborative inquiry can bring together indigenous wisdom with emerging understanding to illuminate new ways forward, and remind us of well-worn paths to change.

I'm thinking right now and writing it down, and someone who reads this may find themselves changed. Or not, because thinking doesn't always get the job done; it can be misguided; it can be self-centered and self-righteous. It can create the opposite effect it purports to desire.

Physical action carries the exact same risks, but thinking can mitigate the risks of action, and action the risks of thinking. Besides, mistaking, limitations and even misuse, for uselessness is never a good idea. Change requires action *and* thinking. Thinking discerns a way forward; action puts feet on the path.

Us

At the height of the pandemic, I noticed a particular use of the word *us* in U.S. historian Heather Cox Richardson's daily newsletter, "Letters from an American." Whenever she wrote about pandemic deaths in the United States, she referred to *us*, as in, "More than 30 million of us have been infected since the pandemic began. And 549,892 of *us* have died." (Italics mine.)[26]

There is power in her choice of that word, especially as some consider lives lost or at risk as acceptable trade-offs for economic stability, or for individual freedoms to not mask or socially distance. The data is clear that most who have died of Covid-19, and those most at risk, are already vulnerable in U.S. social structures: older people, BIPOC people, people with disabilities, people without homes or otherwise financially insecure.

In that context, the choice to say *us* could be described as an activist decision, refusing to characterize those who have died, those who have lost loved ones, and those at greater risk, as *them*. That refusal confronts marginalization, insisting that Richardson's readers consider themselves impacted by lives lost, even if the losses were not close in. Arguably, choosing *us* also invites the reader to some responsibility for that impact.

I agreed with Richardson's use of *us*. I even felt myself approving of it, because I approved of what I saw as the meaning of that choice. If I'm honest, my approval was quietly self-righteous, and here's some irony: with that righteous approval, I separated myself from those who I imagined didn't agree with me. Without even thinking about it, I conjured a *them*.

That realization was humbling, and I tried a little thought experiment. I imagined saying, "Hundreds of *us* stormed the Capital on January 6th, 2021", or "Millions of *us* voted for [the one I didn't vote for.]"

I could easily object and argue that neither statement is true, because I didn't storm the Capitol and I voted the way I voted. Yet here I am writing this piece, very much alive, and I didn't object to Richardson's assertion that well over half a million of us have died of Covid.

Why is that?

Certainly some who stormed the capitol are among those more vulnerable to Covid-19, and the odds are that some of their loved ones are among the dead. The same must be true for people who voted differently than I, some of whom, no doubt, later died of the virus themselves. So, *they* are among the *us* of whom Richardson writes.

What would happen if I believed the sentences in my thought experiment, if I seriously embraced as *us* those whose experiences, beliefs, behaviors, and perspectives vary wildly from mine, even people who would do violence to those with whom they don't agree, including, perhaps, me? How would that change my day-to-day, or my actions in the conscious service of social justice, equity, and nonviolence?

The word *us* in a simple sentence speaks volumes about choices to extend care or to withhold it. Choosing to extend or withhold care is arguably a political decision. I mean political, here, not in the electoral or government sense. I mean understanding where power and influence lie in general, and choosing to use or confront power in the service of change. There is power in my choice of words, even tiny ones like *us*.

I don't think choosing to consider myself part of an us necessarily implies alignment with differences that amount to violence and injustice. I think it implies that the essential well-being of each one of us matters to me. That simple level of care can lead to understanding, compassion, the possibility of relationship. History offers plenty to suggest that understanding, compassion, and relationship—on balance with a stalwart insistence on justice and nonviolence—is indeed a powerful recipe for change.

False Consensus

Audre Lorde was a well-known and highly regarded poet and activist when she was invited to speak on a panel at the New York University Institute for Humanities Conference in 1979. Her talk was just under three pages long, but is remembered widely for one short sentence, "For the master's tools will never dismantle the master's house."[27]

Lorde's reference to enslavers was meant as a metaphor for all systems that limit social equity and liberation—oppressive systems. Beyond that, much has been written, especially since Lorde's death in 1992, about the meaning of those words.

Very often though, those ten words are used as what activist and writer Micah White calls, "the atomic bomb of discussion enders." White's concern is the seemingly endless list of strategies for change that get labeled as the master's tools, including, for example language, art, and commerce. "If the master's tools cannot be appropriated," he continues, then, "in an age [when] capitalist masters claim ownership over everything, only resignation is possible."

"It is tragically ironic," White writes, "that a saying originally intended to be a revolutionary tool has come to play a reactionary shutdown role [that] limits our options to act boldly."[28]

In his discussion of this misinterpretation of Lorde's intent, Micah White introduced me to the term "false consensus." It's a useful term, I think, for a compelling idea or opinion that has hardened into a widely held belief so cherished that any digression is met with disdain and dismissal at best, and violence at worst.

For me, every activist decision has got to be based on what will most likely get the job done in the context of history, vision, and the current moment. And here's the thing about history, vision, and even the current moment: they change. There is always more to learn about the past; every current moment reveals new understanding; and the irrepressible fact of change constantly unfurls an emerging future.

So any consensus is also subject to change, and potentially false in the light of careful thinking. But consensus is born of community and certainty, and community and certainty promise rest and safety, and human beings require both. So the common retreat to false consensus, and even its fierce defense, make sense.

To be clear, Audre Lorde was serious about the need to watch out for the master's tools, warning, "They may allow us temporarily to beat him at his own game, but they will never enable us to bring about genuine change." She was also clear about the need to examine assumptions, and keep in mind that the role of community is not, "a shedding of our differences, nor the pathetic pretense that these differences do not exist."

Lorde was speaking in this instance to white feminists of the time who were resisting, dismissing, and attempting to silence Black women's challenges to the feminist consensus of the day. But her words apply, I think, to any rejection of a new way forward on basis of consensus only.

False consensus can be avoided with careful, critical, collective thinking in response to every new understanding, every turn of the moment, every gift of insight from an emerging future. Such thinking is a threat to certainty, yes, but thoughtlessness is the enemy of liberation.

Lorde would seem to agree. Just before she spoke those ten now-famous words, she said, "survival is... learning how to stand alone, unpopular, and sometimes reviled, and how to make common cause with those others identified as outside the structures in order to define and seek a world in which we can all flourish. It is learning how to take our differences and make them strengths."

Standing outside of consensus, making common cause with others, making our differences strengths, those too will call consensus and certainties into question. As frightening as it may be to step out of those retreats, I think it's the only path to the creativity, collaboration, and courage required to act boldly for "a world in which we can all flourish."

Imperfect and Necessary Practice

Practice, as I understand it, is specific behavior repeated with informed intention for a particular kind of change. The intention I hold for social change is a world in which more and more people thrive, with less and less violence. My personal practice proceeds from there.

It's easy to start a reflection on practice with the famous admonition to "Be the change you wish to see in the world." I used to see this on bumper stickers a lot; now it shows up in internet memes. When it is attributed at all, it is attributed to Indian lawyer and nonviolent activist Mohandas K. Gandhi.

Actually though, Gandhi never wrote or said this. Here's what he actually wrote:

> "If we could change ourselves, the tendencies in the world would also change. As a man [sic] changes his own nature, so does the attitude of the world change towards him. This is the divine mystery supreme. A wonderful thing it is and the source of our happiness. We need not wait to see what others do."[29]

Hold on to that. Here's another thing about Gandhi: he was in his youth an unapologetic racist, though he is widely seen as renouncing that position later, even by many accounts becoming a staunch anti-racism advocate. And an anti-sexism advocate, though he chose to test his own sexual restraint by sleeping naked with a young niece—arguably a gender and power—insensitive decision, at best.

In a 2019 National Public Radio piece on the occasion of Gandhi's birthday, journalist Lauren Frayer reported that, "many Black Africans are calling Gandhi a racist. #MeToo activists are questioning his sexual practices." Frayer also reminded readers of Gandhi's friend and colleague, and India's first Prime Minister, Jawaharlal Nehru's plea to "keep [Gandhi] human… Gandhiji was a great man, but he had his weaknesses, his moods and his failings… Gandhiji was much too human and complex to be [a god]."[30]

Mohandas Gandhi was not perfect; that is clear. It's also clear that his life was defined by a personal practice directly linked to the change he wished to see. So practice does not, as conventional wisdom goes, make perfect.

But practice can make…better. Systems science holds that when part of a system changes, the system itself always shifts. That's as much the case with forest ecology as it is with human systems, which are made mostly of interactions and relationships. So the ways we behave with one another, when undertaken repeatedly with intention, can yield small and large shifts in the systems of which we are part.

Gandhi wrote, "If we could change ourselves, the tendencies in the world would also change." Change, though, is just that—change. It's not perfection; it's not even an imperfect endpoint. It's a direction. I have no illusions that my practice or anyone else's will result in the end of all violence and a perfectly equitable world. Still, I try to align my practice with change in that direction.

The reason liberatory change requires practice, though, is that we are human and therefore vulnerable to all sorts of moral blunders. Great icons of social change are no exception and neither, certainly, am I. Ask some of my current and former colleagues and friends. Ask my stepchildren. Ask my siblings. Ask my life partner. I fail often. When I do there is nothing for it but humility, self-investigation, accountability, and returning to the work of living my intention.

That is the nature of practice, after all. The fundamental discipline of practice is returning over and over again to action with intention. Successful practice is evidenced by failure and increase; one step back is as essential as two steps forward.

I have often heard people say, in light of the news of the world, "We can't all be activists. I don't know what to do." Intentional practice offers a path from that discouraged place; relationship by relationship, interaction by interaction, each person can make change, even if only in small ways.

When I'm stalled by not knowing my place in creating the change I seek, returning to practice, just changing myself, lifts my spirits. Then—a small miracle—I often find I can do more. Perhaps this is what Gandhi meant when he wrote of, "a mystery supreme... A wonderful thing it is and the source of our happiness. We need not wait to see what others do."

Transformative Power of a Single Word

I am a word nerd. I once sat past midnight with some poet friends in graduate school, reading the names for various groups of animals from a dictionary, exclaiming with actual glee over a pandemonium of parrots, a smack of jellyfish, a bloat of hippos. Seriously, we were at it for hours.

Those kinds of words are worth a chuckle, and then I move on. Other words are stop signs at T-intersections, the kind of words that require me to turn. Lately I'm noticing more of these.

I'm thinking for example of the word, repair and its extension, reparation, which in general terms means to make things right after a wrong. The case for social reparation is not new; it's in the Hebrew bible, for example, specifically referring to reparations for slavery and caste.

Although the United States originally promised reparations ("40 acres and mule") for slavery, those promises were not kept. Michigan member of Congress John Conyers introduced a bill just to study reparations at every session of Congress for thirty years, before it was taken up in 2021.

The word reparations has recently come into more public prominence, with both serious consideration and renewed resistance to the possibility of reparations for colonization, genocide, and slavery in the U.S. Writer and journalist Ta-Nehisi Coates makes what I consider a deeply compelling case for this kind of reparation in a 2014 essay in *The Atlantic* magazine. When Coates uses the word reparations, he means, "the full acceptance of our collective biography and its consequences... more than recompense for past injustices." Coates continues, "What I am talking about is a national reckoning that would lead to spiritual renewal."[31]

Reckoning is a word that stopped me some time back and made me turn, and has driven my behavior since. So reparation as a part of reckoning has caught my attention and caused me to wonder what it would mean for my own behavior to be reparative. I have to stop and think: What would it mean for me to behave in a way that addresses past injustices and contributes to a reckoning that leads to spiritual renewal? What would it mean for the organization I work with to be a reparative organization?

See? One word, "reparation" was a stop sign, and required a turn.

Another word that has stopped me and required me to rethink my actions is extraction. On its own, this word just means removing something, for instance in terms of chemistry, as in extracting one part of a compound from the whole. The nonprofit Climate Nexus defines extraction in a social justice context as, "removing value from its environment, exporting it for use mainly by the elite of *Western* (white) economies, and discarding it when finished."[32]

The word extraction used in this way applies even to social change work itself. For example, as organizations recognize a need to make systems more equitable, a market opens for social change insight. Arguably, there's nothing wrong with that on its face, but social change insight is often hard-won through the challenging and even tragic experiences of communities deeply affected by injustice. If those insights are commodified and sold without consent from and benefit to communities where the insights were forged, then social change strategy itself becomes extractive.

Stop sign. The organization I lead is in the business of learning, and creating change strategies based on that learning. We need to be very careful about extraction.

Reparation and extraction are old words that I see differently in a social change context. Completely new words, especially those created with intention, can also stop me in my tracks. My colleague Jordan Laney introduced me to one such word recently, Affrilachian.

The poet, multi-disciplinary artist, activist, and teacher Frank X. Walker coined the word Affrilachian over a decade ago. Walker was at a conference for Appalachian writers, and noted that he was one of two Black writers in attendance. Checking a dictionary, Walker saw that the word "Appalachians" specifically referred to White people who live in the Appalachian Mountain region of the U.S.

So he made up a word to make Black poets and artists of the region visible. In the years since, a whole movement, area of study, and communities of artists have emerged around just that one word. Since Jordan introduced me to the word Affrilachian, I've discovered poets and artists who have challenged my thinking and introduced me to new perspectives. I'm starting to see how those challenges will require me to turn.

A new word opens a window where there was a wall. An old word is a sturdy boat, carrying me across a river I didn't know I needed to cross.

If this is a transformative time, and I believe it is, then I want to know as much as I can about the places from which transformation can come. A single word is often such a place.

MORE REFLECTIONS ON FEAR

"They literally met on two sides of the street."

That was a friend and colleague of mine, a devoted educator and social equity advocate. In his Midwest town, on the same night, at the same time, two different groups met to talk about school equity. In a building on one side of the street were people organizing for racial equity in the town's public schools. In a different building, on the other side of the street, people were organizing to resist those efforts. The thing is, my colleague said, "They were seeing two completely different realities."

My friend and I share the same basic ideas about how these different perspectives came to be. But what's to be done, we wondered, to keep the street from getting wider and wider? If my intention is to increase social equity and decrease violence, to help make it possible for more people and the planet to thrive, what's the most effective way to respond to the people across the street from me?

Later I posed that question to another good friend, also a long-time educator. "Fear," she said, without hesitation, "We need to deal with the fear."

I believe that others' emotions cannot be opposed. I can disagree with an idea, an opinion, or a statement of fact. I can wish someone else didn't feel what they feel, but I can't disagree that they feel what they feel. I can't disagree that they are afraid.

People learn what to fear from both experience and information, though, and this is where it gets confusing, because I can disagree with information. So if another's fear is rooted in information with which I disagree, can't I start there? Can't I try to convince them that their fear is wrong because the information on which it's based is wrong?

I can try, but it's doubtful that I'll succeed. Rational conversation and logic are no match for beliefs that underlie fear because fear's purpose is to protect from threats that feel existential, as in: If this thing happens, I might not be who I am. I might not have what I need to survive. I might die. So I will hang on tight to my fear, thank you very much!

In terms of social change, this is a problem, because when fear drives behavior that puts others' well-being and even lives at risk, it's time to take deliberate and urgent action to mitigate that fear.

But too often that urgent action takes the form of devaluing fear: Disagreeing with fear. Screaming at fear. Taunting or belittling fear. And in response, fear digs in harder.

Strategies for responding to fear need to cause fear to diminish, not dig in. What fear needs in order to recede is reassurance. Also information, but not in the form of argument. In order for fear to stand down, the information that a fearful person needs is, "I will not hurt you." or "I will not let you be hurt."

In the interest of liberatory change, challenging others' fears is not an effective option. But setting that option aside must not mean giving up on responding to fear; fear lights matches every day, touches them to gas, and sets the world on fire. Those fires have got to be put out; the match-lighting fiercely resisted. Doing that will require learning to respond to fear.

When I am tempted to talk someone out of their fear (won't work) or devalue their fear (makes it worse), it's because I myself am afraid, and often with good reason. My fear is a good alert system. When it gets me out of the way of a fast-moving train, it's a good motivator for quick action.

But social transformation is not a fast-moving train, transformative strategy requires careful thinking, and careful thinking isn't possible when fear is in charge. My fear is most useful when I pay attention to its alert with appreciation and respect, then set it aside so I can think and then act.

So that's where my work begins, and where I'll return over and over again. As I get better at seeing and soothing my own fears, I'll be more able to respond to others' fears in ways that leave room for those fears to step aside. That's one way to keep the street from getting wider.

Just Dance

When I consider my place in movements for social change, I generally conjure sentences strung together to try to make sense. When I write in this way, I'm thinking out loud, and I deeply believe in the necessity of that thinking, of considering complexity and finding ways to comprehend it. In late June of 2021, though, I was stunned by the ambition and beauty of a wave of new projects by friends who are dancers, musicians, poets, and playwrights. Seeing and reading their work, I realized I'd been forgetting something; as precious as they are, sentences are not enough.

Sentences are not enough to reflect and relate to the ineffable complexity of people, cultures, histories, and the planet. They're not enough to encourage a beautiful world. I'd been forgetting the power of making—making paintings and gardens and graffiti; bouquets, baskets, and gorgeous meals; poems, melodies, shapes, and movements.

Realizing what I'd forgotten, I asked my friend Danielle Boutet—a visual artist, musician, writer, and professor of art and spirituality—to think with me. I began by asking what her thoughts were on art as a way of making change. She stopped me right there: The idea that a person can make social change, she reminded me, is ridiculous, because social change exists with or without our efforts. Change just is. It can no more be made than the sun on my face as I sit here and write.

We kept talking, reminding ourselves also that change is infinite, that any attempt to put a period on change will not succeed. I can decide to apply myself to the effort of bending the famous moral arc toward justice, but it's not like bending a bar toward the ground. The bar will meet the ground, and the job will be done. That's not so with the arc of social change, because the future is a shapeshifter. All I can do is stay curious, determined, and humble, applying my intentional actions to affecting the direction of change.

But what of action without an intention for change? What of art with no thought of a moral arc at all? Danielle considered the question, and answered, "If work is moving and full of light or even darkness, if it's full of humanity," then that is more than enough. No intention is required, we decided, for art to contribute to the collective work of infinite change.

Danielle reminded me of what the visionary artist Laurie Anderson has often called "the beautiful and strange," and of something Anderson once said about art, "If given a choice between something I thought was politically, let's say, 'correct,' and something that was very beautiful and strange, I would choose the second."[33]

I came to that conversation thinking about art as activism. I left considering the beautiful and strange for their own sake, as reflections and generators of a beautiful and strange world. It's a whole other way of relating to change, as infinite and inevitable. Our participation is essential, and our intentions matter, but they're not always necessary and sometimes they get in the way.

There's one more story to bring this home. When my stepchildren were young, they enrolled in a hip-hop dance class. After the first class, their mom asked if the instructor had added context to the class. Had they learned about the history of hip-hop? Its importance in African American culture? My stepdaughter, who was nine or ten at the time, sighed. "Mama," she said, "we just want to dance."

ON RIGHTOUS ANGER

I often find myself both affirming anger and feeling deeply uncomfortable with its expression. That tension is worth exploring, I think, because in the interest of liberatory change, anger is both invaluable and precarious.

I didn't grow up comfortable with anger, but came to value it as a young adult, largely informed as I often was then (and still am now), by the poet and activist Audre Lorde. "Focused with precision," Lorde said in a 1981 speech, "anger can become a powerful source of energy serving progress and change."[34]

I understand the necessity of anger in the work of increasing equity. As paradoxical as it may seem, I recognize the role of rage in the work of decreasing violence. Anger insists on my attention. It requires me to see. Without the sharp light of anger, I might not summon the courage to act. Lorde writes, "When we turn from anger we turn from insight, saying we will accept only the designs already known, deadly and safely familiar."

So why am I troubled by anger at all? Why do I call it precarious? I circle back to Lorde. There's a call for transforming anger in her words. In the service of change, she writes, anger doesn't generate power on its own; it requires translation, focus, and precision.

Precision has come to be associated with accuracy, but the word in English comes from the Latin, praecidere, to cut off. What must be cut off from anger to make it precise? I believe what needs trimming is self-righteousness.

There is a fundamental difference, I think, between righteous and self-righteous anger. I appreciate writer and musician Sara Haile-Mariam's definition of righteous anger, which she describes as "an anger that lets you know when your boundaries have been crossed. Anger in response to mistreatment, to being asked to shrink. Anger born from injustice. This anger always comes to reveal when your circumstances are misaligned with your worth... It says these circumstances do not reflect my wholeness and the truth of who we are."[35]

Mariam's illustration of injustice is helpful to me: "circumstances misaligned with [essential human] worth." Righteous anger is fueled by a sense of injustice. Self-righteous anger is fueled by a sense of moral superiority.

That difference matters, at least in the context of efforts for liberatory change. Moral superiority can very easily excuse or lead to actions that deny others' essential humanity. In Mariam's illustration, that's injustice.

I'll circle back to Audre Lorde again. In the next sentence after she spoke of the power of anger focused with precision, Lorde said, "And when I speak of change, I do not mean a simple switch of positions or a temporary lessening of tensions, nor the ability to smile or feel good. I am speaking of a basic and radical alteration in those assumptions underlining our lives."

I can't see how anger fueled by moral superiority, which arguably works against justice, will benefit any effort toward changing the assumptions underlying injustice.

This is not a theoretical discussion. I'm frustrated with calls for liberation that affect the opposite for those with whom the callers disagree, or which only serve to increase resistance. Unleashing self-righteous anger often looks like name-calling, denigration, and marginalization. It's easy to post an angry meme calling those who deny climate change idiots, but I have to ask, to what end?

One more circle back to Audre Lorde (for now). Such imprecise anger, she argued, will only result in guilt at best and defensiveness, even sharp resistance, at worst. "Guilt and defensiveness," Lorde wrote, "are bricks in a wall against which we all flounder; they serve none of our futures."

I don't see the purpose of angry responses that serve none of our futures, and this explains my discomfort with some expressions of anger, to an extent. Buddhist teacher and activist Lama Rod Owens seems to share my impatience when he writes, "In activist communities, our relationship to anger is immature, ill informed, and overly romanticized."[36]

But Owens' answer to that concern reveals another source of my discomfort. He agrees with the value of anger in the service of change, arguing compellingly for the necessary energy anger provides. But that won't be available, says Owens, without tending to emotions that underlie anger. "When I am taking care of my hurt," he writes, "the energy of anger becomes an energy that helps me cut through distractions and focus on the work that needs to get done." Likewise, Owens continues, "If we refuse to acknowledge our hurt… we will never be fully empowered in our agency to channel the energy into clarity and directness while reducing harm."

If anger is not reducing harm, and especially if it is causing harm, then anger is no friend to liberation. Righteous anger, though, and anger strengthened by tending to other emotions, provides essential energy for doing the work that needs to get done.

It has not escaped me that Audre Lorde spoke in 1981 of the need for precise and focused anger, and that almost forty years later Lama Rod Owens writes of the need to "cut through distractions" and "focus the work." Clearly these lessons are hard to learn. So I turn back to practice, knowing that practice necessarily includes mistakes and setbacks, committing to honing my own anger to serve the work of liberatory change.

QUESTIONS INSTEAD OF ANSWERS

Freedom is a concept both deeply held and very, very broadly understood. To be free means profoundly different things to different individuals, and in different cultural contexts. I can imagine a circle of a hundred people, defining freedom one at a time, each one baffled by the others' definitions.

People have always been willing to lay down their lives for freedoms to and freedoms from. But human beings have never worked out their differences about what it means to be free. Over and over again, these differences violently collide.

My understanding of violence (I mean, here, between humans) begins with words that ignore the complexity of one human being, or assume universal sameness within any group that shares just a few characteristics. Violence is a moving sidewalk; dehumanizing belief, long or briefly held, is the ticket to that track. And my reading of history and observation of the world tells me that always, immediately or eventually, violence begets more violence.

So I'm left with a deeply challenging conundrum: If your idea of freedom means you will work hard to limit or eliminate my idea of freedom, and if resisting with violence is not an option, then how do I respond?

I'm stopping here to tell you what just happened: The first time I typed that last line, I wrote, "If resisting with violence is not an option, then how do I protect my freedom?" I thought about that for a minute, and I changed it to, "how do I respond?" The first ending invites a cycle of antagonism, a constant grapple to prevail. The second invites the possibility of change.

This piece is not about freedom. In fact, if you try an internet search for the word "freedom," I advise setting a timer first, or asking a friend to be ready to pull you out of the infinite rabbit hole in which you'll find yourself. I don't believe humans will ever agree on the nature of freedom.

But I'll work for liberation anyway. I want to work for more and more people to have access to more of what they need in order to exercise their full capability, well and safe from violence. The way to that increase isn't necessarily answers. I don't believe we'll inform one another into liberation. Questions, though, really good questions, may help clear the way.

Comedian and writer Hannah Gadsby has said about facing the contradictions in her own life, "I could not understand it, that is, until I could." She's also said that questions hold way more wisdom than answers. Without good questions, not understanding creates a stalemate. Good questions are the bridge between, "I could not understand," and "I could."[37]

The question, "How do I respond?" when others' freedoms might limit mine invites possibilities beyond protecting my own perspective. It lets in more light. The more open the question, the more honest I am that I sincerely don't yet understand. The more I admit that I sincerely do not understand, and the more I learn to bear that state of not understanding, the more likely I am to grow calm enough to frame the questions that could lead to liberatory change.

Hannah Gadsby again: "My struggle is not to escape the storm, my struggle is to find the eye of the storm as best I can."

The eye is the calmest part of the storm, but it's still the storm. That storm—the differences between humans—is not going away. I don't believe ideas like freedom can be beaten or convinced into submission. Ideas and beliefs can change, but they're held firm for a reason; threats and even opposing certainties will only tighten that grip. Questions though, sincere, and open-hearted questions, can and have caused ideas to stand down, or shift enough to make more room for more people to thrive.

Practicing Complexity

In December of 2021, while our holiday dinner warmed in the oven and our families laughed in the other room, my good friend and I leaned against the kitchen counters and talked. She and I share a concern about certainty, and rigid perspectives about paths to change. After we'd talked a while about these things, my friend said, "It's all about complexity."

Recognizing complexity, accepting complexity, tolerating, and even appreciating complexity. This is one of the most essential practices of the work of liberatory change, and among the most difficult.

I understand complexity as a lot of moving parts, relating to, and affecting each other in many ways, changing all the time. Complexity is by its nature confusing, sometimes chaotic, usually troublesome, and almost always challenging.

In my work, I usually think in terms of complex systems—organizations, networks, and communities of all sizes. But what if I apply those definitions to individual people? What if I recognized, tolerated, even celebrated their complexity?

Like many, I mourned the passing of Archbishop Desmond Tutu that year. I had been moved and inspired for decades by Tutu's unwavering commitment to nonviolence and human rights, by his practiced faith, and his apparent kindness, all of which I aspire to in my own life and work.

And Desmond Tutu was complex. He was the revered Bishop of Johannesburg, then Archbishop of Cape Town, described by one writer as an "entertaining, excitable, impish little man." A devoted

Christian, irritated by tardiness to times for prayer, Tutu also once said that if he got to heaven and found there a homophobic god, he would rather spend eternity in "the other place."

When Tutu died, Heads of State around the world mourned the loss of a "moral giant." Also, one prominent South African social change leader remembered Tutu as a "Black elitist," who had, "abandoned the Black majority to enjoy the material comforts of the post-[apartheid] era."[38]

I can choose to ignore the parts of Desmond Tutu with which I'm uncomfortable. I can choose to let those diminish his light in my eyes. Or I can nod and say, of course; of course he was complex.

I choose that nod. I choose to practice recognizing, tolerating, even celebrating complexity. I choose to see people whole, or at least to assume they are much more than the parts I see. When I can, I choose to find common ground even as I am honest about my disagreements or discomfort.

That's not hard, for me, with Desmond Tutu, because I don't live in the complex political history of South Africa. It is very, very hard for me when I think of many political leaders in my own country, and when I consider its history. Patrick Gaspard, the Director of the Center for American Progress, reflected on the complexity of the United States in that regard, when he said, "There is an unmistakable history of brutality towards Black people in this country that was legal, systemic and tied to profit systems... and that legacy continues to be manifesting in so many ways."

Then he continued, "But what's also undeniable is the fact that America has made a journey at every level of society to push through that."[39]

When Gaspard served as a U.S. diplomat in South Africa, he was often asked how the U.S. could take a moral position on human rights, given its history and present conditions. Gaspard's response was that "it was actually because of that history that we had a perspective that was unique, that gave us a sense of what we could contribute to the broader conversation of rights in the world and what it means to promote and then protect the interests of the most vulnerable in society."

It's not one or the other for Gaspard, it's both. It seems to me that his recognition of the complexity of US history offers more pathways forward. He doesn't deny its past or present brutality, or the work to push through and even overcome that brutality, or the possibility of turning its lessons to strength in the larger work of the world.

Holding all of that, it seems to me, opens more pathways to change.

As tempting as it is to reduce people and systems to their parts, I believe people cherish their own complexity. I know when my own complexity is challenged, when I am seen as only one or a few things, and especially when stereotypes are attached to them, boy do I bristle. I'm not at all inclined, in those instances, to appreciate the complexity of the other. I don't even feel like sitting next to them.

I imagine that others feel the same, and where does that get us?

If I want to be an agent of liberatory change, it's imperative that I resist actions and ideas that limit the possibility of people and planet thriving, even living. And just as importantly, I don't think I get to reduce any human being to their parts, especially their stereotyped parts. I don't think I get to use the power of my position or personality to cause them great harm. That will only lead to more harm, which is not in the interest of a more equitable and nonviolent future.

Resisting the impulse to dismiss complexity is very, very hard, most of the time. So it's a practice—I'll keep trying and failing and trying again—but it's a critical practice.

When I was growing up there was a little ceramic plaque on the kitchen wall of our house, an Amish saying, "Don't throw the baby out with the bathwater." I didn't know it then, but that was a lesson in complexity. The formidable challenge of recognizing, tolerating, and celebrating complexity is to do something about the dirty bathwater, and at the same time, cherish the baby.

If I don't, I can practically hear doors closing on the possibility of change.

Troubling Questions

"What do we owe one another?"

This was the last of three questions that ended a January 2022 essay in *The New Yorker*, by physician and researcher Dhruv Khullar. Khullar was wondering on the page about ways to navigate an enduring Covid-19 endemic. He also asked, "What level of disease are we willing to accept?" and "What is the purpose of further restrictions?"

Khullar referred to these questions as complex, and they are just as they stand. But when I begin to pull them apart their complexity deepens: To whom is Khullar referring when he writes the word, *we*? Does this undefined group factor cultural and political differences into their answers? What if you're willing to accept a level of disease that I'm not willing to accept? How will I avoid getting sick? What if your restrictions seriously inhibit my capacity to thrive?

I'll be honest, these questions scare me. But does that mean they shouldn't be asked?

Recently, a dear friend of mine cried as she said to me, "Can we even ask questions anymore?" My friend has always considered herself progressive, literally, and politically. She's found belonging among those who question the status quo. As the pandemic took hold, she'd asked earnest questions about intersections between capitalism and medicine, about the tensions between collective well-being and harmful isolation. She wondered aloud about the lack of attention to all the ways, besides a vaccine, to take collective care of each other in a pandemic.

Asking those questions lost her friends, drove her to isolation, left her open to harsh judgments and social media name-calling from the community to which she had long felt she belonged. All that was before she came out as having decided against mandatory applications of Covid vaccines, deciding instead to take up other ways to mitigate the possibility of harm for herself, her family and, importantly to her, for others.

My friend understands that her critics were afraid. She understands their fear and respects their decisions. And she's also afraid. She's afraid of systemic greed, and of tightly held truths devolving to tyranny.

I'll be honest, her questions scared me, too. They pointed to too many doors I was afraid to open, and threatened to topple ideas I'd counted on to be sturdy. But I love my friend, and I trust her, so I sat with my fear and asked her to tell me more. In the end, though we have answered her questions differently, I'm no longer afraid of them. In fact, they have widened my vision.

But I see that others find her questions dangerous, and so in the service of careful thinking, I need to ask, is there such a thing as a dangerous question? A quick online search reveals what I suspected; I'm far from the first person to ask that question, and the answers are as various as you can imagine.

I'm not going to try to tender a definition of dangerous questions of my own. I'm more concerned with the liberatory worth of punishing those who ask questions that seem dangerous, because they elicit fear.

When questions spark fear, it feels like trouble. Fear demands attention from the fearful, and deserves it, I think, but giving attention is different than giving power.

Attention says to fear, I appreciate your warning, I'm on alert, I've got this; you can sit down now.

Giving fear power says, do whatever you need to do to make the threat go away. The problem with that is that questions—even scary questions, maybe especially scary questions—are absolutely necessary tools for liberatory change. Transformation thrives on questions.

When questions spark fear, it feels like trouble. When questions are forbidden on pain of punishment, we're in trouble.

So how to navigate the arguably real possibility of harm in questions? How to convince fear to stand down?

Activist and writer adrienne maree brown writes, "While all harms are not equal, even the most heinous require a way home... we must become more and more comfortable with what is wild in each of us. The contradictions, the ways suffering shapes who we are... "[40]

brown is writing in the context of the contemporary Abolitionist movement, advocating for a shift away from punishment (e.g., prisons), to deep accountability. She's lovingly calling on her colleagues in the movement to reconsider their own punitive behavior toward each other, and toward those with whom the movement has differences.

I think there are some answers in brown's words to Dhruv Khullar's question, "What do we owe one another?" (I mean we, here, universally.) Even if I can't shake a conviction that a question is harmful, it seems to me that a commitment to liberatory change requires me to do the work to become more comfortable with the questioner, the wild in them, the contradictions, the real possibility that their suffering shapes their concerns.

But I'm working on shaking my fear of questions as much as I can, because, for me, as uncomfortable as I get with some questions, as genuinely threatened as I sometimes feel, I'll take all that in the service of a transforming world.

The River or the Fire

In early March of 2022, as the Russian invasion of Ukraine began in full force, I found myself scrolling too much. I skimmed five different newspapers online each day. I listened to podcasts. I glanced at front page photos on grocery store news racks that I usually ignore. Early on, one of those photographs—of a Ukrainian mother and children killed by mortar as they dashed across a bridge, their small pet unscathed in a carrier nearby—nearly brought me to my knees. I'd been reading that news story as I walked to my car. When I got in, I put my head on the steering wheel and cried.

Later that day news came from a friend that people of color escaping the violence in Ukraine were being ignored, or worse, refused when they reached the border. Not everyone in those lines of people holding signs of welcome invited Black and brown refugees into their homes.

I thought of the complicity of consumption and disingenuous geopolitics that fueled this war. I saw that the bias of the media is driven by the bias of its consumers, of which I am one. I read about the unthinkable invasion of a sovereign nation—as I sit in my office on land invaded and stolen from a sovereign nation.[41]

I understand that I am haunted by this particular war, in great part, because those bombed-out neighborhoods look like places I have lived. Because teenaged skateboarders with three days of training are on their bellies with automatic rifles behind sandbags in Kyiv, while ten miles down the road from me, my beloved teenaged nephew rides his skateboard to school.

And I have been haunted not nearly enough by other boys fighting other wars who remind other women of their beloveds. I sit with accountability for that.

Back and forth; but this, but that. I have been struggling this way with myself since this invasion began. Such struggle is useful when it leads me to clarity, leads me to change, not so much when it ties me in knots. So as the war began, I worked frantically to think myself free, to understand what, if any, responsibility I had to act in response to this particular war. I fretted about the work in which I was engaged: research and learning to find strategies for more equitable schools and organizations, writing about liberatory change, collaborating with others engaged in similar pursuits. Should I stop that, I wondered, and focus on Ukraine or some other conflict?

But in my close-to-frantic search for what to do, I almost forgot that liberation has two conditions, singular and ongoing, and there is no need to choose between the two.

Singular liberations are observable events or obvious shifts. It's clear to see that something definable has ended or begun. In the long, collective, global haul, though, liberation doesn't work that way. It's never-ending. Its essence is change.

Like all change, liberatory change is a river, winding and rewinding its way through the course of human history, meeting obstacles, carving switchbacks, changing direction but always, always urging itself toward the sea. To join that change requires constant, critical attention and thought, revealing, and confronting past and present violence, injustice, and inequity over and over again. That work is never finished because there will always be obstacles, including and arguably most of all, in the complex, flawed nature of human beings.

Singular liberation is like a boat on fire, requiring sharply time-sensitive action, and focused on the end of a specific violence, confinement, or threat, and immediate relief and support to its victims.

If I close my eyes, I can see that river. I can also see boats on fire. I don't have to choose, I mustn't choose, between tending the river and the fire. If I can help put it out, I will. If not, I'll do all I can for those on that boat. Neither action will stop the river from flowing, but if I do nothing, I'm left with a river of fire.

WHEN I AM TIRED

Sometimes I just get tired. Weary of socio-political differences with friends, colleagues, and family. Worried about climate change. Deeply despairing of war and its impact. Exhausted by the relentless loss of livelihood and life to hate and bias and bigotry. Dismayed by what sometimes feels like a crumbling of the planet and of people's capacity for humanity. Impatient with the pace of change. Discouraged when change turns back on itself, and we have to start over again.

I wake up on those days, or look up from reading the latest news, and think, I just want to put this all down. But I know the work of liberatory change is a lifelong haul for me, and a generations long haul for the world. Putting it down is not an option for people whose dignity and well-being—whose very lives, are at stake. So it's not an option for me.

Still, my weariness and the vital necessity of change do battle in my head. One day when that battle was raging, I gave up and took a walk. I looked at the sky. I paid attention to the ground under my feet. I tried to breathe more slowly. As I calmed down, it came to me that there are three things I can always do, even when I am tired, that will respond to the urgency of the moment:

I can rest.

In the context of my committed intention, I can slow down, breathe deeply, and rest for as long as I need to in order to be well and get back to work that requires more energy.

Tricia Hersey founded The Nap Ministry to affirm, as she says over and over again, that rest is resistance. This mantra is rooted in her own experience, "As a Black woman in America, suffering from generational exhaustion and racial trauma always was a political refusal and social justice uprising within my body. I took to rest and naps and slowing down as a way to save my life, resist the systems telling me to do more... This is about more than naps."[42]

Activists Lucky Kogugabe and Iris Nxumalo-De Smidt echo Hersey when they write "Rest is political... a resource that replenishes us, supports us to transition from surviving to thriving, and enables us to honour our movements and ourselves." Resting as part of collective effort is particularly critical, they write, "more consolidated, healthy, creative and moving at the speed of trust."[43]

I can slow down and reflect.

I can remind myself that I am living in a moment with thousands of years of working for change behind it, and a future of change beyond my existence. I can remember, as Rabbi David Wolpe writes, "that human beings are capable of transformation" with regular reflection on their own behavior and amends.[44]

Nonviolence and restorative justice teacher Kazu Haga warns that changemakers are "much likelier to perpetuate the same systems of violence that we are trying to resist when we work in a frenzied pace."[45]

I can abstain from violence.

I can for example refrain from posting on social media until I have the energy to channel my anger strategically, without name-calling or otherwise denigrating others' humanity. I can cancel meetings with people whose ideas or behaviors scare or anger me, until I can respond nonviolently. Not being violent takes energy, but not as much, I've found, in the context of rest and reflection. And abstaining from violence is always a critical strategy in response to the urgency of the moment.

I can rest. I can reflect. I can always abstain from violence. Not just because I am tired, but because caring for myself is a liberatory act, preserving my own small Light in the world, and the gifts I can offer to the work of liberatory change.

I just stopped typing, looked out my window, and took a deep breath. Now I'll go on with my day.

CIRCLES OF ACTION

I was invited to a small gathering of women for tea and good conversation, though two of the women there refrained from tea because they were fasting for Ramadan. One of them needed to leave the gathering early; it was time to break the fast at her home in Qatar.

This was a virtual gathering; I sipped my tea from my home in Vermont, the only participant in the U.S. Others sipped theirs in nine different countries in South America, East Asia, India, Europe, and the Middle East.

The hour began with an inspiring, ten-minute talk offered by Dr. Rana Dajani, a molecular biologist and professor at Hashemite University in Jordan, and an advocate for global women's rights. The conversation that followed was remarkable in many ways, not least this: At the end of the gathering, almost to a person, we said some version of, "Thank you, all. You changed me today."

While everyone who was on that call is committed to social change, I doubt that anyone came with activist intentions for the call itself. Yet, without our knowing it would, that video-gathering became a circle of action.

Change in any part of a system perturbs the system to change. That's as true in human systems as it is in a forest. In human systems, intentional action can perturb a system to change in intended ways. Small actions in carefully chosen parts of a system, often called leverage points, can provoke large, systemic shifts.[46] These understandings form the foundation of systems practice, whether undertaken by activists, advocates, organizational leaders, or consultants.

But not everyone has access to the power that comes with recognized leadership, certainly not everyone is a paid consultant, or has the means to hire one; and for many, activism and advocacy are out of reach.

Such was the case, it would seem, for Austrian psychiatrist Victor Frankl, when he and his family were imprisoned in German concentration camps during World War II. Frankl's father, mother, brother, and wife did not survive. Frankl lived to write about his experience in the bestselling *Man's Search for Meaning*, in which he offered this insight, "Everything can be taken from a man [sic] but one thing: the last of the human freedoms—to choose one's attitude in any given set of circumstances, to choose one's own way."[47]

South African freedom fighter and then President, Nelson Mandela echoed Frankl when he wrote in *Long Walk to Freedom* that he and his comrades in prison "drew strength and sustenance from the knowledge that we were part of a greater humanity than our jailers could claim."[48] During his 28-year imprisonment, much of it brutal, Mandela also famously insisted on treating his jailors with respect for their full humanity, writing later that "To be free is not merely to cast off one's chains, but to live in a way that respects and enhances the freedom of others." By their own report, some of his guards changed their political views as a result of Mandela's behavior toward them, some even helped smuggle his writings to the outside world.[49]

Mandela found a circle of action sleeping in a six-by-six cell at night and laboring by hand in a hot quarry by day; Frankl in the brutal conditions of German concentration camps as his loved ones and friends died around him. As a result, by their descriptions, the systems that imprisoned them shifted: slivers of thriving where there had been none, small diminutions in violence, a few particular liberations.

Bless the activists, absolutely. I am grateful to the organizers, the earnest elected, the risk-taking radicals who push at the edges to make room for more people and the planet to thrive. And their work is not the only way to perturb a system to change.

If I sink into believing the only path to change is to be that kind of activist, then I risk missing opportunities to do what I can in my own circles of action.

"Everything can be taken from (a person) but one thing: the last of the human freedoms—to choose one's attitude in any given set of circumstances, to choose one's own way."

As much as it pains me to say it sometimes, I am a part of the systems that both heal and plague the world. No one can stop me from acting "in a way that respects and enhances the freedom of others." My actions in even the smallest of systems—circles of action—within larger systems can perturb them to change.

With few exceptions, no one is powerless; everyone has a circle of action. The only decision is how to live in them.

NEW WAYS TO SPEAK FOR PEACE

Arguing rarely changes minds. Harvard business professor and writer Arthur C. Brooks makes this point when he asks, "What is the point of arguing with someone who disagrees with you? Presumably, you would like them to change their mind. But that's easier said than done: Research shows that changing minds, especially changing beliefs that are tied strongly to people's identity, is extremely difficult."

Brooks goes on to describe such disagreements as the "sorts of fights that might give everyone involved some short-term satisfaction—they deserve it because I am right and they are evil!—but odds are that neither camp is having any effect on the other; on the contrary, the attacks make opponents dig in deeper."[50]

Brooks isn't alone in that estimation. Social psychologists have long identified and continue to affirm the "boomerang effect," finding over and over again that insults and degradation reliably deepen and increase the strength of opposing positions. Recent research on politically motivated argument suggests that those positions are often tightly aligned with identity and belonging; they are tribal. Disagreements, especially when they devolve to insult, are heard as threats to self, family, and community, to belonging itself. In addition to hardening positions, such threats are often met with life-threatening or life-ending violence.[51]

Indeed, Brooks suggests, "Disagreements can feel like a war in which the fighters dig trenches on either side of any issue and launch their beliefs back and forth like grenades. You wouldn't blame anyone involved for feeling as if they're under fire, and no one is likely to change their mind when they're being attacked."

So why do people engage in arguments in which they attempt to change each other's minds? The people I know share the experience affirmed by research—no one wins, nothing changes. Yet they happen over and over again, and can get nasty fast, even at the slightest whiff they're about to happen. One afternoon at my local garage, I chatted lightly about politics with a friend who worked there. Overhearing our conversation, his colleague—who I'd not yet met—came out of her office and demanded I defend a position she assumed I had (She was right, though I hadn't said a thing about it before she popped out of her office.) I responded with something like, "I can see that's upsetting to you," and backed out of the door. It was clear to me that argument would get us nowhere.

Brooks suggests people argue for short-term satisfaction, for some degree of affirmation of the rightness of each party's position. I suspect it's deeper than that. I suspect those arguments that feel like battles happen because the arguers are afraid, or enraged, or heartbroken, or all three.

I often get into these kinds of arguments—in my head. I argue with Russian military leaders, with elected officials banning math books that dare to mention race, with those who would call me a pedophile and a groomer because I am a lesbian. I argued hard with the police officer who'd shot another unarmed Black man from behind at a traffic stop.

But I kept those arguments in my head. I share my rage and grief with three close colleagues. I cry with my partner. I channel my fury into my work, which is all about driving the changes I demand in those arguments in my head.

I don't always succeed at that kind of discipline. I have tossed my share of verbal grenades. I have gotten better at calling out inhumanity without being inhumane myself, but it still takes work. I imagine it always will.

In April of 1967, Martin Luther King spoke to a church full of people in New York, inviting them to choose between nonviolent coexistence or violent coannihilation.[52] He was talking about the war in Vietnam, making the moral case that the movement for civil rights join the movement against the war. I believe the choice he offered applies to arguments as well. I have a choice to reach for nonviolent coexistence or to verbally annihilate the other's humanity.

For me, that choice is both simple and hard. It's simple because I firmly believe that it's strategically unsound to hurl insults in the service of a less violent future. It's hard because I feel threatened myself; I feel afraid, and fear makes it tough to think creatively about how to engage difference.

At that same sermon at Riverside Church, Dr. King declared, "We must find new ways to speak for peace." Fighting bitterly in a fruitless attempt to change each other's minds does not work, I'm committed to not doing it anymore. Instead, I'll heed King's call from over half a century ago, and keep searching for new ways to speak for peace.

What Are You Willing to Do?

"We are not just hurt. We are angry. We are mad. This shouldn't have happened. We do our best to be good citizens, to be good people. We believe in God. We trust in him. We treat people with decency. And we love even our enemies. You expect us to keep doing this over and over again, forgive and forget… What are we supposed to do with all this anger and all this pain?… This is not just some story to drive the news cycle. This is our mother, this is our lives… Help us change this, this can't keep happening. I say to you, what are you willing to do?"[53]
– Garnell W. Whitfield, former Buffalo, NY fire commissioner, and one of Ruth Whitfield's four children.

Ruth Whitfield was murdered, along with 10 other Black shoppers and employees, by a self-proclaimed white nationalist on May 14, 2022. In the days after her murder, Ruth Whitfield's children and grandchildren asked the question over and over again, with tears running down their faces, "What are you willing to do?"

One week later, Buffalo pastor George Nicholas, Buffalo resident and urban scholar Henry Louis Taylor, sociologist Adolphus Belk, and historian Kathleen Belew offered more possibilities for action than I could keep track of as I listened to their conversation on the radio program, *1A*.[54]

They outlined actions for politicians, church leaders, and local civic leaders. They spoke of necessary action in housing, zoning, food, and health policy. They called for critical examination of connections between white nationalism and efforts to suppress teaching history and civics. They pointed out the eerie similarity between the "manifestos" of white nationalist mass murderers, and emerging mainstream political rhetoric, and called out critical work of ensuring the vote, and informing the voters.

But the anguished question asked by Ruth Whitfield's grieving family was not, What can be done? It was, What are you willing to do?

To change the course of history will require a historic stepping up, every person who cares about liberatory change assessing their skills, talents, relationships, and time, and deciding to put what they find in themselves to use. It will require resilience, in some cases no small amount of courage and creativity—and will.

Will is a strong cloth woven of intention, decision, determination, and persistence. It is founded on yearning, aspiration, and desire. When I ask myself what I am willing to do, I mean what do I *want* to do, not what I *can* do.

That's a stern conversation to have with myself. It makes me be honest, and accountable to the changes I say I want to see in the world. The question of what I can do is related but separate. Once I honestly assess my capacities, I have to assess my will: How much of what I have to give am I willing to give? Once I've ensured that I'll have enough rest and food and water and shelter and health, how much will I lean on the arc of justice? How much of my money, skill, time, or body will I give to that effort? How much will I step up?

For some that will mean standing in line for hours to vote. Others will stand for election. Others will stand in the streets. Some will teach, some will write, some will sing or make art. Some will only be able to speak to their neighbor. Some will only be able to pray.

After the shooting in Buffalo, Ruth Whitfield's granddaughter Simone Crawley posted on her social media page, "Every one of you knows that you have a personal choice to make."[55] That is a choice predicated on will, so before I step up, I'll step back and re-ask the question, "What am I willing to do?"

No More Time For All of That

Writer, editor, and social commentator Roxanne Gay has no patience with civility, which she describes as "the idea that if everyone is mannered enough, any impasse or difference of opinion can be bridged." She challenges this idea hard, "If you want to talk about incivility," she writes, "let us be clear about how deep those roots reach," pointing out a cycle of state-sponsored and supported violence that goes back centuries.

Gay is making a case for rage, and dismisses calls for civility that would silence it. "If we dare to protest, if we dare to express our rage, if we dare to say enough," she writes, "we are lectured about the importance of civility. We are told to stay calm."

"The greatest of American disgraces," Gay says, "is knowing that no amount of rage or protest or devastation or loss will change anything about this country's relationship to guns or life."[56]

Gay means this as an indictment of what she calls "a craven political system" that has failed to act to stop the epidemic of mass violence in the U.S. But I'm struck by a different read of this phrase, "no amount of rage or protest or devastation or loss will change anything about this country's relationship to guns or life." I agree, but for me, that agreement implies hope.

My hope lies in action beyond rage and protest, beyond acknowledging the absolute horror in places like Uvalde, Buffalo, and Newtown.

Please don't misunderstand; I make myself read the stories of the children and teachers who lost their lives at Robb Elementary in Uvalde Texas, my own, acute, remote grief just a whiff of the mountain of grief in that town. I'm still trembling about the carnage in Buffalo. I still weep for the 21 dead at Sandy Hook School. I'm not interested in a civility that means tamping down any of that. I am stony with rage.

But my rage is not reserved for the systems and leaders who fail to act. I also rage against rigid thinking and self-righteousness–the arms folded, my-way-or-no-way stance of people at all points on the political spectrum in response to the latest horror.

There's just no more time for all that.

"No one wins in that scenario," writes adrienne maree brown, "seeking to dominate others leads to contention, violence, and a disconnection from reality."

And yet so much of the response to each wrenching tragedy amounts to pointing fingers: My way is better than your way, or worse, I and mine are better human beings—more moral, more deserving to thrive, than you and yours.

brown makes her case for another way, "internal accountability," which she describes simply as, "Let me act in alignment with my values." Without this kind of individual, internal accountability, brown argues, "nothing really changes... if I act like I care about equal rights for everyone, but internally I believe I hold a superior position to one group of people, that internal superiority will find a way to surface." And that, brown argues, will only continue cycles of harm.[57]

This kind of internal alignment is a lesser-known aspect of Satyagraha, the practice of nonviolent resistance introduced by Indian lawyer and political activist Mohandas Gandhi. In her exploration of Gandhi's philosophy of conflict, philosopher Joan Bondurant reminded readers of his injunction that those who practice Satyagraha, called Satyagrahi, "must consciously examine his (sic) own position, for his opponent may be closer to the truth than he is," and that Gandhi had often spoken of the requirement that Satyagrahi, "maintain an unceasingly open approach" to those with whom they differed.[58]

Toward the end of his life, Gandhi was criticized for speaking and acting differently than he had during the time of resistance to British rule. "But the fact of the matter is," he objected, "that conditions have changed... and I have reacted to that as a Satyagrahi."

There's a thread of accountability here, curving the pointing finger back to ask: Am I acting in alignment with my values? With the future I want to see? Do I examine my own position? Do I leave open the possibility that I'm not right? Am I allowing myself to be changed as conditions change?

None of this is about civility. It's not about standing down, or standing by, or accepting things as they are.

But Roxanne Gay said it herself: "No amount of rage or protest or devastation or loss" will change this country. adrienne maree brown would seem to agree: "The most likely outcome of our currently ruptured society is that humans go extinct." She goes on to say, "I want us to continue as long as we are meant to, which I believe means breaking cycles of harm."

Someday, I believe, stories will be told about this horrible time when teachers died shielding their students from gunshots, when Black grandmothers were murdered in grocery aisles, and Asian grandmothers on city streets. But degrading others' moral positions will do nothing to stop the slaughter. Disconnection and rigid ideas have not worked so far, and I don't believe they ever will.

We will only see the backside of this moment if we do things differently. Beyond stalled arguments and power-plays about who's right, certainly beyond mere civility, there are other paths forward to find. For me, there is way too much at stake not to consider my own agency in that equation, to think harder, and align my actions with the future I want to see.

PRACTICING RESTORATION

It had been a good summer for me. The days were full of productive work. On warm evenings, I took a canoe to a local pond. The gardens at our house came alive with hummingbirds. I often stopped working just to take it all in. When I did, I could feel myself settling down.

Still, despite my own personal calm, I fought dismay about the news. One day as I sat at my desk in Vermont, wildfires burned thousands of acres in California. One raged just a mile from my sister's home. She sent me a photo that day of the things she'd gathered to take with her if she had to evacuate.

It was a small collection: one suitcase, a tote, a box of papers, a basket of special things. I recognized the basket; I have one just like it. Years ago, my parents gave each of us a basket my father had spray-painted blue, replicas of the original "blue basket" in our childhood home. One of us would be assigned the chore of gathering misplaced things into the basket, then we'd carry it around the house, returning each item to where it belonged. In that way, my mother restored the house to tidiness.

In carefully setting aside the small pile of things she'd save from a fire, my sister imagined a different kind of restoration, not returning to life as it was before a fire, but having enough to make a new life whole.

A deepening understanding of restoration like this—facing forward, rather than returning things to the way they had been, helps me stay steady in the face of even the most troubling news of the day.

To restore is generally understood as bringing something back to the way it was, returning to something known. In terms of social change, for some, restoration means going back to a time they believe was better than now. But as facilitator, teacher, and writer Prentiss Hemphill has said, "There is no magical return," no "unblemished time in history" to return to. Instead, Hemphill asks, "We're here now, what do we have to do?"[59]

For me, the answer to that question lies in part in an understanding of restoration rooted in ancient, indigenous practices of peacemaking. Indigenous leaders have chosen to share those practices, and they have evolved into movements for restorative justice. Iterations of restorative justice have been renamed restorative practice, transforming schools and communities, and to some extent organizations.

I've learned to see restoration differently thanks to this history, these movements, and from restorative practitioners. I've come to understand that if I want to contribute to more people thriving, and to an increasingly peaceful world, then I need to develop a personal restorative practice.

But what does that look like in everyday life?

Robert Yazzie, Chief Justice emeritus of the Navajo Nation Supreme Court, suggests that restorative practice begins with compassion. That means, he says, hearing the stories and perspectives of others. Yazzie emphasizes restoring stable relationship, which is not necessarily predicated on agreement. Instead, peacemaking relies on accountability.[60]

In restorative justice and practice, accountability is about seeing and responding to harm. In a personal practice, that means responding to the harms I cause and those from which I've benefitted with what activist Mia Mingus has outlined as the four parts of accountability: self-reflection, apology, repair, and changed behavior.[61]

You'll notice that admitting or assigning guilt is not on that list. Guilt is part of a punitive paradigm. Punishment requires retribution and disconnection. But in centuries of peacemaking, says Robert Yazzie, relationship has mattered more than all else.

That's profoundly challenging for me. I don't necessarily want relationships with people whose beliefs and actions frighten, anger, even harm me. But Yazzie speaks of relationship in a broader sense—staying open to the other's full humanity, understanding their story, their point of view.

For me, that leads to another piece of a personal restorative practice, tolerating fear and sadness instead of batting it away with the punitive impulses of guilt and self-righteousness. When I can do that, I have a much better chance of hearing others' stories and understanding their perspectives. At best, then, my compassion grows, and they respond in kind. We find a way to make peace. Or at least that possibility stays open.

It would be naïve, of course, to expect that to happen all the time. There are certainly people determined against restoration, determined against my thriving, determined against peace. Even then, if I stay in relationship enough to understand their story, I am much more able to craft a liberatory strategy in response.

Restorative personal practice begins with compassion, requires accountability, tolerating sorrow and fear, and maintaining connection. It also requires imagination.

Imagination isn't the same as optimism. It doesn't assume bad things won't happen. It doesn't deny the past, and it doesn't deny the present or immediate threats. When my sister prepared to evacuate, she knew the fire was burning and uncontained, and she knew it could well take her home. When she gathered that small pile of things, she was imagining her life whole after a fire. Whole, not the same.

Imagination offers a vision of peaceful connection, and the possibility that people can change. Restorative practices have for millennia rested on that possibility.

One more thing: Ask any committed athlete or musician, and they'll tell you that practice never, ever makes perfect. Practice makes change. Change never stops and neither does practice. Long-time activists and restorative practitioners say it's hard work and failing is guaranteed. When Robert Yazzie says "It takes a lifetime to learn peacemaking," he means no one lives long enough to get it right. But getting it right is not the point. I can only commit to restorative practice in all my relations, even in the smallest ways, and in that way be part of restoring peace.

The Sneaky Reach of
Dehumanization

In September of 2022, forty-nine documented immigrants got on a plane in Texas thinking they were flying to Boston, where jobs and housing were waiting. Instead, they stopped first in Florida, then North Carolina. When they finally landed, they were not in Boston, but on Martha's Vineyard, a tiny island off the coast of Massachusetts with a reputation as a retreat for wealthy liberals. There was no one to greet them there, and no jobs and no housing. Many had no idea where they were.

Florida Governor Ron DeSantis and his team planned and paid for the whole thing, with the support of Texas Governor Greg Abbott. The team lied to the people on the plane, flew them to Florida and North Carolina, then Martha's Vineyard without their consent to make a point that wealthy liberals were glad to leave places like Florida and Texas to manage an influx of immigrants, but wouldn't accept them in their backyard.

That backfired a bit when the Martha's Vineyard community turned out in droves to feed, house, and otherwise care for the bewildered passengers on that plane. Within days, many headed to places like Boston and New York to join family, find jobs and stable housing. But some stayed on, and continue to feel welcome. "I did not even know where Martha's Vineyard was. And now I feel welcomed by everybody here. I'm working, making friends and this is home for me now," one smiling passenger on that plane told a reporter in June 2023, "I don't want to leave."[62]

Reactions to the Florida and Texas governors' gambit were quick and loud in 2022, many applauding them for making a point about immigration, others absolutely appalled. DeSantis himself was unapologetic. He was clear that the human beings on that plane were not on his mind. They were only useful for making a point.

In opinion pieces, letters to the editor, and everyday conversation, liberals, progressives, conservatives, and politically unaligned alike reported feeling disgusted, sickened, and revolted by the dehumanization of those forty-nine people. In the weeks after that flight, there was an outpouring of moral outrage—with dehumanization at its center.

I was right there with them, and I also kept thinking about the sneaky reach of dehumanizing, how even the morally outraged can be nonetheless in its thrall.

Psychologists characterize dehumanization, largely, in two ways. Human beings are regarded and treated as less than human, generally as animals or objects. In the context of this disregard, people are used for financial, strategic, or political ends. At its extreme, some kinds of people are seen as not human at all, worthy, then, of extermination.[63]

Writing for the nonprofit, The Conversation, psychologist Allison Skinner-Dorkenoo worries about what she calls the slippery slope of dehumanization, pointing to myriad studies in which seeing people as non-human emerges as a precursor to harassment, violence, and systemic oppression, and lead to increased public support for torture and indiscriminate acts of war. "I get a bit uneasy," she writes, "when I see these types of insults get normalized."[64]

I think about that when I read and hear good-hearted, earnest, thoughtful proponents of a less violent, more just world, refer to public figures as pigs, asses, even, literally, not human. Is that a step onto Skinner-Dorkenoo's "slippery slope?" I honestly don't know for sure, but I do know it's worth considering.

So is the other, less often considered, form of dehumanization; that is, characterizing groups and individuals only in terms of to some extent real, but merely partial, negative aspects. Thus, for example, and incorrectly: Mormons are seen as only members of polygamist cults. Muslims are seen as only violent jihadists. White men are characterized only by social privilege. In daily life a terrible boss is nothing else but a terrible boss. The disagreeable bus driver is nothing but a jerk.

The trouble with all this is that none of these characterizations can possibly be true—because every single human being is complex, as is every collection of people. Not only that, those complexities represent identities, life stories, and cultures. Denying complexity, especially out loud, feels like an attack and often elicits a like response. It does not serve an intention for more thriving and peaceful systems, or a more thriving and peaceful world.

Dehumanization of this kind is also strategically unsound, because disregarding the inarguable complexity of any group or person means missing opportunities for effecting change. People act out of their whole complex selves. Groups, tribes, and nations are utterly and profoundly complex. Effective resistance, defense, or alliance requires understanding that complexity.

Still, dehumanization is sneaky. Apparently, it literally gets into our heads. *VOX* science and health editor Brian Resnick reports, for example, that neuroscience research at Princeton University indicates, "when we dehumanize others, the regions of our brain associated with disgust turn on and the regions associated with empathy turn off."[65] That's what allowed dozens of people to deceive and use the forty-nine already vulnerable, traumatized human beings who landed in Martha's Vineyard.

But despite all the outrage about their actions, all the people involved in that cruel plan are not as unique as some might think. I've come to believe that, faced with fear, or saturated with certainty, self-righteousness, or rage, anyone is vulnerable to the temptation to dehumanize. It seems to me that accepting that vulnerability, and actively resisting that temptation, is essential to the possibility of liberatory change.

STEELY COMPASSION

In the fall of 2022, my family lost our dog, Izze, who'd arrived as a puppy and lived with us for well over fourteen years. Our kids grew up with this dog, and in many ways, so did my partner and I.

The morning after he died, I went out for my usual walk with our other dog Theo. It was a stunning morning, the field sunlit and sparkling from an overnight rain. Theo, who usually races off and back again, stayed just a few feet away, or so close I could walk with my hand on his head. All through that first walk with just one dog, I was teary.

What I was feeling, of course, was grief, a space in my sky ringed with love.

We'd been flooded with messages the night before, as family and friends affirmed our sadness and wished us all peace. Even those who don't share our family's attachment to dogs, or had recently suffered life-changing loss, who couldn't be blamed for thinking, *Really? A dog?* To a person, they offered compassion.

Tenzin Gyatso, the Dalai Lama, and spiritual leader of Tibetan Buddhists, defines compassion as, "the wish to see others free from suffering." Joining moral and spiritual leaders throughout the course of human history, he also asserts that compassion is necessary, that humanity cannot survive without it.[66]

It seems to me the reason for that is clear: To not have compassion is to wish suffering on others. That will never result in more people thriving or ever more peace.

So I try to practice compassion, aware of the myth that practice makes perfect. It's not hard to practice compassion for people I see as aligned with my beliefs, or for those of whom I'm not afraid. But when I perceive threats to the shape of my life, my ability to work, be housed and healthy, walk safely outside of my home, and care for the people I love? When I see threats to the moral and civic artifacts–like legal rights, laws, and learning–that make all that possible well beyond me? I'll be honest; practicing compassion in the face of any of that is really, really hard. No wonder the Dalai Lama calls compassion "a sign of strength."

I've begun thinking of compassionate practice on a continuum, from soft to steely. Offered to those I love and care about, in whose beliefs and actions I perceive no threat, compassion is hardly an effort. The more threatening our differences, the steelier my compassion must become.

Steely compassion may seem like an oxymoron, because soft compassion is often mistaken for the only kind. Steely compassion is not so feel-good, and it's what is required when faced with threats, and for those who do wish suffering on others, for those who act on that wish. I call it steely because it requires steeling myself against the temptation to be indifferent to others' suffering. It requires a kind of tough discipline of mind and speech, turning a stern, even steely gaze on my own behavior.

Compassion can hold determined resistance to violence, greed, and repression. It does not require playing nice. There is room for rage in a world of compassion. But if in my resistance and even my rage I wish aloud for the suffering of others, or worse, if I act on that wish, then I am part of the problem.

Please don't get me wrong, I believe in the power of soft compassion; it got me through losing Izze, and has held me through far sharper struggles and griefs. Still, because I choose to align my actions with a more thriving and peaceful world, neglecting to practice steely compassion is a luxury I cannot afford.

WHERE DOES THAT LEAVE US?

This work is hard.

I'm thinking about a text exchange I had some time ago with an old friend. We've known each other most of our lives. We end all of our calls with, "I love you." And we know we have different perspectives on social change, politics, and policy. Occasionally I see a post on her feed that raises my eyebrows. I respond, "hmmmmmm." She sends back a heart emoji.

Our latest exchange was different. She told me about an event in her town headlined by a politician with whom she does not agree. "I'm sorry," she wrote, "I know you like this guy, but I can't stand him. He's all about equity but not equality. He's ruining everything I care about."

I wrote back carefully, knowing that such messages can easily be misunderstood. I said that I wanted to hear more, to understand what this was like for her. I said in my view neither party was getting things quite right. I said I too was afraid of losing things I care about. She didn't respond.

My friend and I will be okay. We've weathered harder conversations. But this one made me think. What if I heard those words from someone I didn't care so much about? Would I respond cynically, think to myself, Really? Ruining everything? Isn't that a bit dramatic?

Would I be tempted to trot out my take on the difference between equality and equity? To lecture on history, generational trauma, and poverty? Policies worsening uneven distribution of wealth? Would I point out gross generalizations about political positions? And would any of that do any good?

What if instead, I take statements like that on their face, very true for the people who make them? What if I tend to the grief that must come with feeling so much of worth has been ruined? What if I meet that experience of loss with compassion instead of cynicism? What if I meet concern for equality with curiosity, instead of correction?

I am not the first by any means to suggest that the answer to these questions is this: It may very well not lead to agreement, but it could soften our hearts. It could open a path to peace between us, and to the possibility of ever more peace in the communities we inhabit.

I'm not talking about peace defined by ignoring differences or tolerating bigoted behavior. I mean disagreement without punishment, violence, or threat of either. I mean a shared desire for more people to thrive without violence and behave in ways that others can too, a willingness to work hard for that to be so, and a belief in that possibility.

But because I often believe that the people with whom I disagree threaten to ruin all that I love, the pull is strong to try to make them change. And the thing is, they feel the same about me. Where does that leave us?

Some argue it leaves us to go at each other with words, power, or violence until one of us is forced to change, or just to disappear. Some argue that right as they understand it will win out in the end. But winning that way eventually turns right into wrong.

When my conviction is muddied by fear, when despair threatens my hope for peace, I can easily fall into line with dynamics I know need to change so that more people can thrive. The hard work, for me, is in choosing, again and again, to resist the temptation to overpower or dismiss, and to begin with compassion and curiosity instead. I don't always succeed, but I try, and with practice I'm failing less often.

That seems to me to be the least—and sometimes the most—I can do.

SOMETHING LIKE GRACE

". . . how sad and ordinary every little life, however gilded, can be."
That's the final phrase in an essay by opinion writer Lucy
Mangan in *The Guardian*, a reflection on the British royal family,
particularly the very public rift between the two sons of the current
monarch.

I care about relationships, how they sour, how they repair.
Otherwise, with all else there is to read and think about, a story
about the British royal family is not at the top of my list. What
caught me about Mangan's final line, though, was that I thought it
contained a hint of grace.

Why did I think that?

I grew up understanding grace as bestowed by a god who loved
and affirmed me no matter what. My mother spoke often of "the
Comforter," gratefully certain of a divine, loving presence, especially
in difficult times, and, while my understanding of faith and the
divine has since changed, I think I understand what she was talking
about. I have felt that comfort too.

Any serious study reveals that the concept of grace, though
variously understood, is ubiquitous among people of faith and spirit,
and grace exists in secular thought as well. David Ames, host of the
Graceful Atheist podcast, says grace is "proactive acceptance, love and
caring for our fellow human beings," adding, "There is nothing more
valuable, moral, or ethical than people loving and accepting one
another."[67]

But the grace I felt in that phrase from Lucy Mangan was not that. The full sentence began with Mangan confessing that she feels sorrow "for all that has been done wrong, all that has been lost and how, in the end, how sad and ordinary every little life, however gilded, can be."

I realize it's the "however gilded" that got me. Arguably, that family represents the most gilded of the gilded, the epitome of ancestral wealth, horribly ill-gotten over hundreds of years of colonialism, extraction, and cultural destruction. Still, Mangan sees their suffering, sadness, and loss, and dedicates the last notes of her essay to making space for that in—despite their global fame—their very human, "little" lives.

What I felt in her decision to conclude the essay in that way was not divine grace; Mangan is not a god, and for people of faith and spirit, divine grace is not something people can offer each other. The grace I saw in her writing is like divine grace; it's generous, given freely despite past mistakes and wrongs, despite limitations. And it opens the way for redemption.

I found several examples of this in the work of activist and Smith College Professor Loretta Ross. In a 2021 TED talk, Ross tells a story of a time when she made an incorrect assumption out loud about a student in her class. "I froze in shame," Ross says. "I expected the student to jump down my throat, because misgendering somebody is a really big deal nowadays. And instead, this student looked at me and offered me grace by saying, 'Oh, that's all right, professor. I misgender myself sometimes.'"[68]

How is that grace? Ross doesn't say, but it seems she felt relieved of her shame, forgiven perhaps, with room to join that student in being human, capable of mistakes.

In another context, Ross talks about working with people with whom she disagrees on almost everything. She calls them the "25 percenters," meaning at best they can find only a bit of common ground. By way of example, Ross speaks of people who behave in racist ways and support racist systems, but don't think of themselves as racist.

Her job as an activist with those folks is not, she says, "to convince them they're racist." It's to focus on her observation that "they do think they're good people," and convince them to do good things from that place. Also, says Ross, it's important to "take their fear seriously. If you dismiss their fear, they won't listen."[69]

Writing about that part of Ross's work, journalist Anand Giridharadas calls that grace.[70] I think that's because Ross has taken a generous stance. It doesn't sanction persistent ignorance, bigotry, or harm. It makes room for the good in people to shine. It makes it possible for them to change.

For many people of faith and spirit, divine grace is most importantly redeeming, because in its freely offered and affirming light, they believe they can behave with love and compassion—even if they have not done so well in the past.

What people can give each other is something like that, affirming shared humanity and the possibility of doing better, generously holding space for the future. In a world crying for change, that's an essential and precious gift to give.

THE GIFT OF UNCERTAINTY

Disability rights activist Hale Zukas, who died in November 2022, is remembered as, "a giant" of social change, audacious and relentless, who "didn't let things get in his way." He was among the founders of the World Institute on Disability, co-led countless protests, and flew often from his home in California to Washington, D.C. to lobby for disability rights. Zukas was one of the dozens of other activists with disabilities who famously took over San Francisco's federal building for 26 days in 1977, refusing to leave until the federal government agreed to enforce civil rights for people with disabilities.

He was widely known for his unsurpassed expertise in public transit, transit funding, and urban design, serving as vice-chair of a board that crafted federal accessibility standards in the 1980s. He designed the first curb cuts in the nation and wheelchair–accessible buttons for elevators, and is credited as a "driving force" for accessibility in the San Francisco Bay Area Rapid Transit system.

Recent photographs of Zukas show sparkling eyes and deep creases echoing the smiles of a lifetime. In the wake of his passing, colleagues and admirers remembered those smiles, and Zukas' infectious laugh. And he also had what one friend called "a righteous temper." He could shut down condescension, from people without disabilities who dared to question the expertise of lifelong wheelchair users, with one sharp response.

In the many remembrances that followed his passing, Zukas emerges as an extraordinary organizer and advocate, leaving a legacy of sustained and sustaining change. So, it was especially notable that his physician and friend of over 50 years, Dr. Alan Steinbach, remembered Zukas most for having learned from him, "How to say, 'it seems to me.' rather than 'it is.' "[71]

It seems to me insists that the speaker's perspective matters. Depending on what that perspective is, that can take courage.

It seems to me also qualifies what comes after, signaling that the speaker knows they have only the lens of their own experience, learning, and belief to support what they're about to say. It leaves room for others to fill in how things seem to them. That leaves room for uncertainty, and requires a different kind of courage.

It's hard to leave certainty aside because uncertainty is scary—actually physically scary. Psychologist David Rock goes so far as to say that "Uncertainty feels, to the brain, like a threat to your life." It's natural to respond to that threat with certainty, shutting down the possibility that perspectives, beliefs, and decisions other than one's own could be right.[72]

The problem, suggests public policy and behavioral scientist Morela Hernandez, is that "being certain about the rightness or wrongness of others' decisions leaves little room for us to grow or expand our understanding, not just of other people but of their situations and their circumstances."

Hernandez sympathizes with the challenge of tolerating uncertainty, asking, "How can we entertain an opposing view when the 'right' choice is so clear to us? It's painful to consider why someone would make such a 'wrong' choice. This psychological pain is real."[73]

As applied to social change, I'd argue the pain is not only psychological. Choosing the right path forward, the right idea, analysis, policy, or strategy can mean the difference between whole communities thriving-or not; choosing the right way can have literal life and death implications.

That makes certainty even more attractive, but, paradoxically, says Hernandez, it, "limits our ability to make progress," and can "prevent us from finding a way forward."

To address this paradox, Hernandez suggests building up a

tolerance for uncertainty over time, purposefully and regularly engaging with multiple perspectives. By way of example, she offers an exercise of listening to a media outlet that, "makes you mad. Listen long enough to allow your emotional reaction to stabilize (or subside) so your mind can process what's being said."

Hale Zukas' speech was difficult for most to understand. He often communicated by pointing to letters on a board attached to his wheelchair, using a pointer attached to a helmet on his head. I can only begin to imagine how many times he had to listen to perspectives that made him mad, discounting his prodigious mind, his very right to move through the world.

When she writes about building tolerance for uncertainty in the service of making change, Morela Hernandez invokes a metaphor of a gym workout, conditioning and building physical muscle and flexibility. Zukas' body wasn't built for workouts, but if he could say "it seems to me" so well, then clearly, he'd built another kind of strength, another kind of flexibility.

The world is a richer place for that, I think, where far more people can thrive, because Hale Zukas had the courage to say, "It seems to me."

STEADINESS & ACCOUNTABILITY

Tyre Nichols was a father and husband. He loved skateboarding and photography. He drove for FedEx. On his arm was a tattoo of his mom.[74] On January 7, 2023, when he was twenty-nine years old, he was pulled over by Memphis police who eventually beat him to death. Ensuing investigations revealed that the officers involved had lied about the encounter, and that most of them had belonged to a special squad long known for its racist violence.[75]

Nichols' murder is filled with details that echo countless other killings of young Black and brown people—literally countless, as in uncountable. For hundreds of years murders like these passed without notice outside the communities in which they occurred. Outside the piercing grief of family and friends.

In response to each killing, the chorus rises again, a predictable call and response: Why does this happen? What will we do? Pundits and thinkers and activists will respond with analysis and solutions. Some who sit in places of power can and should take structural, cultural, and political action that could prevent another killing. Some of them will act, some won't. In response, others will organize and agitate, pressuring the powerful.

But what of the vast majority who sit before the tangled mess that drives this madness, having no idea which end of which string to pull? Just sitting helpless invites despair. We can't have that; sustained despair is the enemy of liberating change.

And hope is the enemy of despair, and there's hope in the knowledge that systems change when their parts are changed. And human systems are made of people, behaving among one another. And I can always choose how I behave. I can align my actions with the change I achingly wish to see. In the wake of another killing carried out with vicious impulse and unrestrained indifference to consequence, I can choose the opposites—steadiness and accountability.

When I think of steadiness, I think of the parents and grandparents I've watched respond to a ramping-up child. Gentle, firm voices saying *Hey now, get hold of yourself*. I remember a particular relative at a crowded family gathering, stopping mid-conversation, turning to look toward a ruckus beginning, then saying her child's full name, a quiet laser across the room. Attention secured, she met her child's eyes, and with a subtle shake of her head, settled that child right down.

There was no threat in her look, nor in the other voices I remember, just a wise admonition: steady now. I borrow those voices, breathe deeply, collect my thoughts, consider the impact of my behavior, decide what I'll do with my voice and body next.

I borrow the voices of men in a circle at San Quentin prison, each who had taken a life. One by one we listened as they said: I did this. I took a life. I will tell you the impact that has had, the lives destroyed, the grief. I accept responsibility for that impact. I have taken steps to be sure I can say I commit to not doing that ever again.

But how do I bring those voices into what writer and educator Mia Mingus calls, "the small things between us?" How do I practice accountability in my day-to-day? Mingus offers what she calls deep apology.

I've begun to practice deep apology as a way to be accountable for smaller harms, like when I'm late for a meeting, or forget to respond to an email. And for bigger ones, like when I go sideways in anger, sarcastic instead of forthright. I walk through the steps that Mingus suggests: I say I'm sorry. I say what I did that warrants apology. I name the impact of what I did. I show that I understand that impact. Then I commit to not doing it again.[76]

Practicing steadiness and accountability, in small ways, day -to-day, may seem like a pin drop compared to the roar that Tyre Nichols' killing deserves. But imagine if one of the policemen there that day had been practiced at getting hold of himself. Imagine if those with the power to stop police violence were practiced enough at accountability to accept the horrible consequences of the system of which they're a part, and commit to doing no more harm.

There are many things I can do in the short wake of Tyre Nichols' killing, and the long, long wake of so many others. I can lean hard into the work of the organization I work in, learning what works, then creating and implementing new strategies for change. I can write these small essays and invite others to think along. I can vote, join marches, write letters, urge friends, colleagues, and family to consider change.

Everyone has a list like that. It's not for me to judge their length or what's included in those lists. Except this: barring cognitive limitations, everyone can choose to behave in alignment with the change they ache to see. That fact defies inaction, so it defies despair.

So I reach into the tangled mess and pull on the string of my own behavior. I choose to practice the change I seek. I choose to defy despair.

So Much Depends on Identity

In 1923, physician and poet William Carlos Williams published a little poem, "The Red Wheelbarrow."

So much depends

upon

a red wheel

barrow

glazed with rain

water

beside the white

chickens.

That's it. That's the whole poem. It's widely anthologized and discussed. An internet search about its meaning yields many results. But almost all agree the poem works by drawing both sharp distinctions and painting a whole, familiar scene.

So much depends, the poem seems to say, on holding difference and relatedness at once.

So it is, I think, with the ways people think of themselves in terms of what many call social identity, that is, how people think of themselves and each other in terms of things like race and class, gender, biological sex, religion, physical and mental ability and disability, sexual orientation, ethnicity, nationality, and age.

So much depends on those differences. Social identity grounds culture–music, food, tradition. It makes community, the ease of being with others who see the world through a similar lens, who share history as well as experience of the present day. Social identity helps people understand themselves, gives shape to the way they move through the world.

It's also true that many social identities are constructed rather than objective, often created to serve ill purposes. Consider race: Historians and social scientists have made the case that race was constructed to justify domination, not least enslavement, for economic gain. Historian Nell Irvin Painter says it plainly. "Race is an idea, not a fact."[77]

Recent research underscores those assertions. Vence Bonham, Deputy Director of the National Human Genome Research Institute, summarizes consistent findings. "There is more genetic variation within self-identified racial groups than between them." Increasing numbers of scientists argue for jettisoning concepts of race altogether. Michael Yudell, a professor of public health at Drexel University, says race is a concept "too crude to provide useful information."[78]

Still, there's no denying the shared experience of racism. Anthropologists Audrey and Brian Smedley spell it out, writing, "Race as biology is fiction, racism as a social problem is real."[79]

Race is a fiction, yet racism is real, and so is culture based on the shared history and experience of those who identify with a particular race. Which is fiction.

It gets confusing. But I keep going back to that poem: so much depends on difference and relatedness. Both.

Consider gender and biological sex, persistently conflated but actually very different things. Biologists and geneticists have long known that a significant number of people are born with markers and physical traits that defy characterizations of male and female.

Those facts, writes developmental biologist Claire Ainsworth, "do not sit well in a world in which sex is still defined in binary terms."[80] Stubborn constructions of gender are at odds with biological facts. They're also at odds with historical and changing realities of what it has meant and means to behave as "male" or "female." At odds with emerging expressions of being human that eschew binary gender, or even gender at all.

And yet, to many around the world, sharply drawn definitions of gender are critical to cultural and religious expression, and to intimate understandings of one's place in the world.

So much depends on social identity that losing it can lead to serious depression and anxiety. Social identity offers belonging, connectedness; for many it offers a road map to being human.

Confoundingly for some, social identity is often exclusionary. People who share a social identity, constructed or not, close ranks in communities, social gatherings, and other events. Those who are excluded ask, Why separate when we want a more inclusive world? Aren't we all of the same species, sharing what it means to be human?

It's out of this place that some objections to social identity emerge, when people say things like "I don't see color, I see people." When they say, "You're not a gay person to me, you're just you".

But I've wanted to reply more times than have that I am gay, and I love that. I'm proud of what I have overcome, and what gay people have accomplished together. When I hear, "You're not gay, you're just you," it's a part of me being erased. I don't want to lose that difference between us.

Some scientists would like to see the concept of race dissolved altogether. Some people would like to see gender dissolved as well. John Lennon wrote of a world without religion. But social identity is, for many, as precious as air, though much, much more particular. It's not just a wheelbarrow, it's a red wheelbarrow, glazed with rain. And it's their treasured, glistening, red wheelbarrow.

It's uncomfortable to live with paradox, with things that seem to clash against each other. I struggle to hold the particulars of social identity, especially those that have been constructed precisely to undermine shared humanity. It seems at odds with the world I want to know. But is it?

The world I want to know will affirm difference and relatedness. So, I'll strive to hold them both—because so much depends on it.

WEATHERING

A physician begins with, "At your age…," and misses the infection that's causing my pain.

A middle-aged person who comes to our house to fix an appliance asks, in an effort to make conversation, "What sort of work did you do?" A younger companion takes my elbow in a crosswalk. I look at them, surprised, and move my arm to my side. A newscaster enthuses about a "65-year-old woman" accomplishing regular things like starting a business or heating her house with wood. I yell at the radio, "So what if she's 65?!"

I try to be gracious in the face of increasing bias about my age. Sometimes it's annoying. Sometimes it's truly discouraging. Sometimes, like with that doctor, it's meant months without help for real threats to my well-being. I know most people mean well, but I'm already tired of it.

Then I imagine the volume of my experience turned all the way up. I imagine living in a racialized body, an entire lifetime on alert, generations of ignorance, insult, and far worse. I imagine being transgender and hearing political leaders call for my eradication.

I think of Denver City Council candidate Chris Hinds heaving himself out of his wheelchair onto a debate stage. There was no ramp, and organizers suggested he crawl. Being on that stage was the only way to participate in the debate, and participating in the debate made Hinds eligible for substantial campaign funding from the city. "It was a choice," he said, "between my campaign's viability or my dignity."[81]

Constantly being denied dignity, confronting bigotry, discrimination, and barriers, even bearing threats to one's very existence, is exhausting. It's debilitating. It's literally sickening. And yet, writes public health and social justice scholar Arline Geronimus, it's also ordinary.

Geronimus has been steadily gathering and sharing evidence of this phenomenon for decades, coining the term *weathering* to describe it. Her work has long informed public health policy and activism, and her book, *Weathering: The Extraordinary Stress of Ordinary Life in an Unjust Society*, puts it all together for the first time in a non-academic form.[82]

Geronimus began her work by amassing evidence of illness and death directly linked to weathering for Black Americans. Her book deepens an understanding of the impact of weathering on people of color, as well as others who face chronic discrimination, barriers, and bigotry. One example: Half of rural Kentuckians living in generational poverty will not reach the age of 50 without disability linked to weathering.

The causes of death associated with weathering are not, as is often assumed, addiction or violence. Weathering kills through diseases like cancer or heart disease. It's not eased by self-care or success, either. On the contrary, writes physician Farrah Jarral, the evidence Geronimus presents suggests that "the effects of weathering are even more pronounced for those who exercise grit, resilience and determination in the face of prejudice."[83]

I've gleaned all this from reading reviews, and some of Geronimus' academic work. As I write this, *Weathering* has yet to be released. I'm looking forward to reading it when it is. Meanwhile, I'm reminded that millions of people are moving through life chronically bruised, injured, and ill from injustice.

There's work to do, policy work and structural change, change in education and organizations, in government and community, to address the sources of those injuries, and to heal them. There's also work to do in the every day, person-by-person, especially when those injuries are aggravated by missteps and mistakes, honest ignorance and bias, and by forgetting.

That's brought to mind a mistake I make sometimes, as a sort of metaphor. I forget, or I don't know, that a friend has, for example, an injured shoulder. I sling my arm over that shoulder, or lean in for a hug. When I do, I hurt them. My friend may cry out or speak to me sharply. They may shy away. They might even be mad. That fact that I didn't mean them harm doesn't diminish the pain I've caused.

At my best, I apologize sincerely. If I've forgotten the injury, I apologize for forgetting too. If I honestly didn't know they were injured, I express regret that I didn't know. I assure my friend I won't do it again. If they ask for ice, I go get ice. If they need some space from me, I step aside.

It would do no good to dwell on my intention, or my honest not knowing that shoulder was sore. It would be awful to get mad at them for hurting or to question whether their pain is real.

But that's exactly what happens, far too often, to people who suffer from weathering. When it does, it only makes things worse.

Besides my work, besides advocacy, writing, and teaching, what can I do about weathering? I can continue the work of understanding the impacts of weathering, sharpening what Geronimus calls a "weathering lens," but there are too many injuries to know them all. So, inevitably, I will cause harm. I'll use an incorrect pronoun, or a word I didn't know has a painful cultural history. I'll act on a bias I didn't even know I had.

When I do, I'll resist any impulse to defend myself or my intentions, or worse, to diminish the pain.

I'll remember to offer what harm requires: a focus on the person who is in pain, a sincere apology, compassion, and commitment to not do it again.

THE TROUBLE WITH CONVENIENT
BELIEF

In the wake of another school shooting, which should never have become predictable, the calls predictably came: Ban the guns or control them. Send thoughts and prayers. Blame a particular group or challenge, and focus all energy there.

All of it felt toothless. After I closed my eyes and shook my head; after I said out loud to the empty room, in one breath, oh no; after that, I stared out the window and thought to myself, we have got to do this differently.

What I meant, what I mean, is that when responses to horrible trends and events begin to sound like shouts returning across an empty canyon, echoing themselves but changing little, then it's time to stop shouting and listen.

The poet, thinker, and activist Audre Lorde once wrote, in a poem I cherish,

> Even when they are dangerous examine the heart of those
> machines you hate
> before you discard them.
>
> ....
> Do not pretend to convenient beliefs
> even when they are righteous
> you will never be able to defend your city
> while shouting.[84]

I cherish that poem, "For Each of You", among other reasons, because it has always reminded me to be both humble and fierce in my efforts for change, to avoid resting in convenient beliefs–that is, beliefs that seem obviously right to me, given my own singular and inevitably limited experience. Beliefs so tenacious they prevent me from seeing other ways forward.

I wonder if banning guns has become a too convenient belief, and if I needed to examine the hearts of—or, in this case, the hearts of those who love—the machines I hate.

As if in answer, right around the time three children and three adults were killed by a shooter with an assault rifle at a school in Nashville, Tennessee, the *Washington Post* published a survey of over 400 owners of AR-15 rifles. The piece includes videos of several people explaining why they own those particular guns. On the same day, the *Post* also published a thorough review of the history of automatic rifles in the U.S. and an exploration of its rise in both numbers and cultural prominence.[85]

The role of profit especially, while unsurprising, is laid out here in profound detail. Also, racism and racist backlash, fear, images of war, rigid masculinity and other deeply held identities, gaming culture— these and more, both purposefully manipulated and evolved, have brought the automatic weapon to its current status. One former gun industry executive, now a gun control advocate, says it's become like a "religious relic."

One particular thing that struck me about the survey is that most of the people surveyed, and most of those who spoke on video, did not seem to be cynics. The beliefs or desires that ground their choices to own such a gun are sincere. Some of those beliefs are bewildering or terrifying, to me, but they are nonetheless sincere.

There is no evidence in history or scholarship that deriding sincere belief has any positive effect on social change. In fact, there's ample evidence to the contrary. Yet another predictable response to shootings is exactly that, derision. It rises, always, to absolute sneering disdain.

It's an equal opportunity disdain, for sure, but I'm interested in strategies that will drive down violence and increase thriving, so it's disdain for gun owners and their beliefs to which I'm referring here. Because it doesn't work.

So, there's that, and there's the fact that in the decades since mass school shootings began in the U.S., sticking to a single-minded strategy of insisting on banning automatic rifles, has not yet worked, either. Arguably, it has (I'm deadly serious here. I mean no pun.) backfired.

Because after each shooting, and whenever a gun control advocate comes to power, sales of automatic weapons increase sharply. In fact, President Obama was "mockingly crowned 2009's 'gun salesman of the year'" by a pro-gun news service.

A Smith & Wesson executive explained this simply, saying, "People buy because they are afraid of future legislation." So when calls to ban guns get louder, some people double down and finally buy one, or buy more, because they're afraid they soon won't be able to buy any.

There is plenty of evidence, in the US and elsewhere, that points to fewer guns as an essential and reliably effective strategy for decreasing violence. So banning them seems like an inarguable necessity. But what if that's not possible, at least not yet? How long will people continue to beat only that drum, and the drum of derision, while the killing continues?

I don't believe Lorde ever meant to stop shouting altogether. It's just that it's not enough. Lorde was fierce in her insistence on change that would lead to more liberation. And in that context of that fierceness, she warned: be wary of convenient beliefs, even when they are righteous. Only when I'm wary of my own convenient beliefs am I able to answer Lorde's call to examine the hearts of the feared and hated, and with what I learn there, find paths to change.

I Love You. I See You. We Will Keep Working.

One of my younger nephews occasionally posts a picture or a headline on his Instagram story, something he's concerned about. A captured and badly mistreated elephant. Children at the U.S. border separated from their parents. The name of another young Black man killed by police at a traffic stop.

I text him just so he knows I see his concern. He writes back, "I don't know how to explain it. It's just so insanely crazy that this keeps happening." We wonder together about what to do. He texts, "I don't know."

I put down my phone. I don't know what to say.

I often don't know what to say. I get silenced by grief, overwhelmed by the complexity of what's to be done, stunned by fear for my own dear ones with black and brown skin.

That week when I texted with my nephew, there'd been pummeling news of police violence directed at Black men, including another young man dead. That, after news of another older Asian woman assaulted, slammed to the sidewalk from behind, then ignored by passers-by. And another transgender woman of color—the twelfth, at least, by April that year—murdered. I stumbled through two days in grief that often slid into despair. I wrote to some friends of color, to transgender friends, told them I was heartsick and couldn't imagine how they were feeling, that I was sending my love, that if they needed to sit down, to please know I would stay standing.

Honestly though, I was finding it difficult to stand. One friend, a woman of considerable faith that's kept her strong for 70 years, wrote back and told me she just wanted to stay in bed. I didn't tell her that I wanted to also.

The work of changing the systems that undergird violence and injustice is relentless; the impact of those systems is not only sense-less, it's sense-robbing. A week or two of no new violence offers the barest glimpse of hope, a minute to focus on other things, like spring flowers, maybe, or a delicious meal. Respites are short-lived, though. Sonya Renee Taylor, founder of The Body is Not an Apology movement, writes, "Letting your guard down and being happy, only to see [another] Black death, is heartbreaking. It hurts so much that sometimes I can't feel anything at all."[86]

After I'd set down my phone during that exchange with my nephew, I paced the room with my hand on my chest; my heart actually did hurt. Finally, I picked my phone back up and wrote, "I love you so much. I'm grateful you care about these things. We'll just keep working on it." He sent a heart emoji back.

There's nothing new there, but it's worth repeating: The long arc of justice requires love. It requires appreciating each other, and saying that. It requires persistence.

There is no shortage of writing and resources about love as a force for social change. Philosopher, author, and activist Cornel West has famously and often said, "Justice is what love looks like in public." Activist, writer, and teacher bell hooks writes, "The practice of love is the most powerful antidote to the politics of domination." There's even an online course, for free from Stanford University, called Love as a Force for Social Justice.[87]

It's also just saying out loud, I love you, especially to those whose very lives are most at risk. It's appreciating each other for what we can do, for who we are to one another, for the extent to which we care. Writer and activist adrienne maree brown insists, "We have the capacity to hold each other, serve each other, heal each other, create for and with each other, forgive each other, and liberate ourselves and each other."[88]

Genuine expressions of love and appreciation are not trivial in the work of change; they're essential.

So is persistence. I fumbled for two days that week in a fog, barely able to keep my commitment—as a white, cisgender woman—to persist, as my friends and colleagues of color, and my trans and nonbinary friends, tucked in, curled up, couldn't, in some cases, move.

I didn't know how to move either, but I had to at least respond to that 14-year-old boy I love beyond measure. What came to me to say to him is also what brought me to my senses and back to work: I love you. I see you. We will keep working.

ENDNOTES

1 Marçal, Katrine. "Mystery of the Wheelie Suitcase: How Gender Stereotypes Held Back the History of Invention." *The Guardian.* June 21, 2021.

2 Palca, Joe. "A Texas Team Comes Up with a COVID Vaccine that could be a Game Changer." Goats and Soda. npr.org. January 5, 2022.

3 Vedantam, Shankar. Interview with Phillip Atifa Goff. "Changing Behavior, Not Beliefs." *Hidden Brain* podcast. January 10, 2022.

4 Minnich, Elizabeth K. (2016) *The Evil of Banality: On the Life and Death Importance of Thinking.* Rowman & Littlefield Publishers.

5 Warren, Robert Penn. *Segregation: The Inner Conflict in the South.* U of Georgia Press, 1956. Reissued. 1994.

6 brown, adrienne maree. "wild seed dinner, alburquerque, nm." adriennemareebrown.net. Blog post. June 6, 2013. (a note: brown prefers not to capitalize her name or post titles.)

7 Crumley, Linda Potter (2006) "Social Justice in Interpersonal Relationships." In O. Swartz (Ed.), *Social Justice and Communication Scholarship.* Lawrence Erlbaum Associates Publishers.

8 Johnson, Kate. (2021) *Radical Friendship: Seven Ways to Love Yourself and Find Your People in an Unjust World.* Shambhala.

9 brown, adrienne maree. (2019) *Pleasure Activism: The Politics of Feeling Good.* AK Press.

10 Sanchez, Kiara, David A. Kalkstein, and Gregory M. Walton. "A Threatening Opportunity: The Prospect of Conversations About Race-Related Experiences Between Black and White Friends." *Journal of Personality and Social Psychology.* (2022)

11brown, adrienne maree. "St. Lous Racial Equity Summit 2021 Keynote (notes)." adrienndmareebrown.net. August 6, 2021.

12 Hoon, Chng Huang, Elizabeth Minnich, John Draeger, Johan Geertsema. "In Conversation with Elizabeth Minnich." Teaching and Learning Inquiry 7 (2):51-72. (2019)

13 The Equal Justice Initiative is a U.S. nonprofit "committed to ending mass incarceration and excessive punishment in the United States, to challenging racial and economic injustice, and to protecting basic human rights for the most vulnerable people in American society.

14 Lorde, Audre. (1977) "Poetry is Not a Luxury." *Chrysalis Magazine.* Reissued in *Sister Outsider: Essays and Speeches by Audre Lorde.* Penguin Random House.

15 From a post on the website of the Mashpee-Wampanoag Tribe. Author not named. "Restorative Justice Practices of Native American and Other Indigenous People of North America." mashpeewampanoagtribe-nsn.gov. May 2018.

16 Two organizations with which I'm most familiar that center restorative practice are Roca, Inc in Chelsea, MA and Baltimore, MD; Stronghold based in Oakland, CA. But an internet search will reveal many, many more examples.

17 See Statistica.com, "Countries with the largest number of prisoners per 100,000 of the national population, as of January 2023" and Worldpopulationreview.com, "Safest Countries in the World, 2023."

18 Russell, Tonya. "Post-Election Calls for Unity Are nothing But Toxic Positivity." Think: Opinion, Analysis, Essays. nbcnews.com. November 6, 2020.

19 Quoted in "Unity Without Justice Is Dangerous, Historians Say." Dasia Moore. *The Boston Globe*. January 16, 2021.

20 Giridharadas, Anand. "We Are Falling on Our Face Because We Are Jumping So High: A Dash of Perspective in a Dark Hour." The.ink/ January 15 , 2021.

21 By way of example: "How Hope Can Keep You Happier and Healthier." Everett Worthington, Jr. *Greater Good Magazine*. June 17, 2020; "The Health Benefits of Hope." Andrea Bonier. *Psychology Today*, online. March 31, 2020; "Why Hope Matters: Rethinking Motivation." Nancy Snow. University of Colorado Academic Advising and Coaching website; "Why Hope Matters Now" interview with Shane Lopez. *Gallup Business Journal* Online. June 25, 2009; "Hope Is Not a Strategy." Mark Jewell. Selling Energy.com.

22 Gay, Roxanne. "The Case Against Hope." *The New York Times*. June 6, 2019.

23 Stevenson, Bryan. Interviewed by Krista Tippet. "Finding the Courage for What's Redemptive." *On Being* podcast. December 3, 2020.

24 Johnson, Tre. "When Black People are in Pain, White People Just Join Book Clubs." *Washington Post*. Outlook. June 11, 2020.

25 Minnich, Elizabeth K. (2004) *Transforming Knowledge. 2nd Edition*. Temple University Press.

26 Richardson, Heather Cox. *Letters from an American*. March 29, 2021. Substack.com.

27 Lorde, Audre. "The Master's Tools Will Never Dismantle the Master's House." (1984, 2007) In *Sister Outsider: Essays and Speeches*. Penguin Random House.

28 White, Micah. "The Master's Tools. The Wisdom of Audre Lorde." ActivistGraduateSchool.org. Undated.

29 Gandhi, Mahatma. *In Indian Opinion* (1913) See also Soschner, Chris. "Gandhi Didn't Actually Ever Say, 'Be the Change You Want to See in the World.' Here's the Real Quote..." Illumination-Curated, posted on Medium. April 4, 2021.

30 Frayer, Lauren. "Gandhi Is Deeply Revered, But His Attitudes on Race and Sex Are Under Scrutiny." National Public Radio. October 2, 2019.

31 Coates, Ta-Nehisi. "The Case for Reparations." *The Atlantic*. June 14, 2014.

32 "Climate Change, Racism, Patriarch, and Policy: Climate Justice Explained." ClimateNexus.org Undated. No author specified.

33 La Frenais, Rob. (1984) "An Interview with Laurie Anderson" in: G. Battcock and R. Nickas (eds.), *The Art of Performance: A Critical Anthology* (NY: E. P. Dutton Inc.) Also: Readers fluent in French who are drawn to Anderson's perspective may find interesting: Boutet, Danielle. (2023) *L'intelligence de l'art: Regard sur les principes organisateurs de l'expérience artistique.* University of Quebec Press.

34 Lorde, Audre. (1981) "The Uses of Anger." Speech to the Third Annual National Women's Studies Association. *Women's Studies Quarterly*. Available at CUNY Academic Works.

35 Haile-Mariam, Sara. "Righteous Anger vs. Entitled Anger." Medium. com. July 11, 2018.

36 Owens, Rod. (2000) *Love and Rage*. Shambhala Books.

37 Gadsby, Hannah. "Three Ideas. Three Contradictions. Or Not." TEDtalks.com. (2019)

38 Uys, Stanley and Dan van der Vat. "The Most Reverend Desmond

Tutu Obituary." *The Guardian*. December 26, 2021; Myeni, Thabi. "'Touched many of us'": South Africans Mourn Desmond Tutu's Death." *Al Jazeera*. December 21, 2021.

39 Smith, David. "Radically Optimistic: The Think Tank Chief Who Thinks the U.S. can 'Self-correct'". *The Guardian*. December 26, 2021.

40 brown, adrienne maree. (2020) *We Will Not Cancel Us*. AK Press.

41 I live in what is now called Vermont, on the western side of the Wabanaki confederacy, which stretches east through New Hampshire and Maine, north into southern Quebec, and south into Massachusetts and Rhode Island. The people of the Abenaki Nation of the Wabanaki Confederacy have lived in this region for over 12,000 continuous years, though between roughly 1600 and 1900 their land was taken, and numbers were decimated by estimated 95% as a result of imported disease, war, and colonization. Abenaki people who remained in what is now called the United States after that were also subject to forced sterilization and pregnancy termination policies in Vermont in the early 20th century. This acknowledgment important and not enough; I'm committed to learning and practicing reparation, and stewarding the land.

42 Hersey, Tricia. (2022) *Rest is Resistance*. Little, Brown, Spark.

43 Kubugaba, Lucky and Iris Nxumalo-de Smidt. "Rest as a Form of Justice in Our Movements." CoFemBlog. Undated.

44 Wolpe, David. " A Rabbi's Guide on Making Amends and Letting Those Grudges Go." *The New York Times*. September 12, 2021.

45 Haga, Kazu. "The Urgency of Slowing Down." Waging Nonviolence. org. January 25, 2017.

46 While leverage points are now broadly applied in systems practice, American environmental scientist Donella (Dana) Meadows proposed the concept in "Leverage Points: Places to Intervene in a System" published by the Sustainability Institute in 1999.

47 Frankl, Viktor E. (1946) *Man's Search for Meaning: An Introduction to Logotherapy*. Reissued 2014. Beacon Press.

48 Mandela, Nelson. (1995) *Long Walk to Freedom: The Autobiography of Nelson Mandela*. Back Bay Books, and "Nelson Mandela Reflects on Working Toward Peace." ArchitectsofPeace.org. Undated.

49 Meldrum, Andrew. "The Guard Who Really was Mandela's Friend. *The Guardian*. May 19, 2007.

50 Brooks, Arthur C. "A Gentler, Better Way to Change Minds." *The Atlantic*. April 7, 2022.

51 Abelson, Robert P. and James C. Miller. "Negative Persuasion via Personal Insult." Journal of Experimental Social Psychology. October 1967.

52 King, Martin Luther. "Beyond Vietnam. A Time to Break the Silence." Sermon at Riverside Church. NYC. April 4, 1967.

53 Spina, Matthew. "Ruth Whitfield's Grieving Family Says a Tragedy Like This Shouldn't Happen Again." *The Buffalo News*. May 16, 2022.

54 "Buffalo's Black community is reeling after being targeted by a mass shooting." 1A. Radio Broadcast. Jenn White, Host. May 17, 2022.

55 Crawley, Simone. Personal Linked In Page.

56 Gay, Roxanne. "Don't Talk to Me About 'Civility.' On Tuesday Morning Those Children Were Alive." *New York Times*. Opinion. May 25, 2022.

57 brown, adrienne maree. "Murmurations: Accountability Begins Within." *Yes! Magazine*. May 31, 2022.

58 Bondurant, Joan V. (1958, rev. 1988) *Conquest of Violence: The Gandhian Philosophy of Conflict*. Princeton University Press.

59 Hemphill, Prentiss. Interviewed by Ayana Young. "Prentiss

Hemphill On Choosing Belonging." *For the Wild*. Podcast. July 28, 2021.

60 Yazzie, Robert. In "About Peacemaking." Video. Indigenous Peacemaking Institute. Peacemaking.narf.org. September 2016.

61 Mingus, Mia. "The Four Parts of Accountability & How To Give A Genuine Apology." *Leaving Evidence*. Blog post. December 18, 2019.

62 Sandoval, Edgar. "How Migrants Flown to Martha's Vineyard Came to Call It Home." *The New York Times*. June 28, 2023.

63 Luft, Aliza. "Dehumanization and the Normalization of Violence: It's Not What You Think." *Items: Insights from the Social Sciences*. May 21, 2019.

64 Abrams, Joel. "The Slippery Slope of Dehumanizing Language." TheConversation.com. June 4, 2018.

65 Resnick, Brian. "The Dark Psychology of Dehumanization, Explained." Vox.com. March 7, 2017.

66 Gyatso, Tenzin, the 14th Dalai Lama. Acceptance Speech, on the occasion of the award of the Nobel Peace Prize in Oslo, Norway. December 10, 1989.

67 Ames, David. "Secular Grace." Graceful Athiest.com. October 26, 2016.

68 Ross, Loretta J. "Don't Call People Out, Call them In." TEDMonterey. TED.org. August 2021.

69 Ross, Loretta J. Quoted in Giridharadas, Anand. (2022) *The Persuaders At the Front Lines for Hearts, Minds and Democracy*. Penguin Random House.

70 ibid.

71 Leon, Joan and Pam Mendelsohn. "Remembering Hale Zukas,

Daring Visionary of the Disability rights Movement." *Berkeleyside Nonprofit News*. December 6, 2022. Erin McCormick " 'Disability is not a tragedy' ": The Remarkable Life of Activist and Rebel Hale Zukas. *The Guardian*. January 8, 2023. Eliyahu Kamisher. "Making BART Accessible: Hale Zukas Pioneered National Disability Rights from His Zooming Wheelchair in Berkeley." The Mercury News. December 27, 2022.

72 Rock, David. "A Hunger for Certainty." *Psychology Today* online. October 25, 2009.

73 Hernandez, Morela. "The Problem with Uncertainty." *MIT Sloan Management Review*. September 15, 2021.

74 ABCstaff. Associated Press. "Who was Tyre Nichols? What we know about man killed after traffic stop in Memphis." www.localmemphis.com. January 27, 2023.

75 Franklin. Jonathan. "The City of Memphis says it has completed its investigation into Tyre Nichols' death." NPR.Com. March 7, 2023; Rick Rojas, Neelam Bohra and Eliza Fawcett. "What We Know About Tyre Nichols's Lethal Encounter With Memphis Police." *New York Times*. February 23, 2023.

76 Mingus, Mia. "The Four Parts of Accountability & How to Give a Genuine Apology." *Leaving Evidence*. Blog. December 18, 2019.

77 Painter, Nell Irvin. (2010) *The History of White People*. W.W. Norton.

78 Bonham, Vence. National Human Genome Research Institute website. www.genome.gov/genetics-glossary/Race; Megan Gannon. "Race is a Social Construct, Scientists Argue." Scientific American online. February 5, 2016.

79 Smedley, Audrey and Brian Smedley. "Race As Biology Is Fiction, Racism as a Social Problem is Real: Anthropological and Historical Perspectives on the Social Construction of Race." *American Psychologist*.

January 2005.

80 Ainsworth, Claire. "Sex Redefined: The Idea of 2 Sexes is Overly Simplistic." Scientific American: Nature. Online. October 22, 2018.

81 Swanson, Conrad. " 'Humiliating': Denver City Council candidate had to crawl on debate stage due to lack of wheelchair access." The Denver Post. February 15, 2023.

82 Geronimus, Arline. (2023) Weathering: The Extraordinary Stress of Ordinary Life in an Unjust Society. Hatchett Book Group.

83 Farral, Farrah. "Review: Weathering by Arline Geronimus: How Discrimination Makes You Sick." The Guardian. March 17, 2023.

84 Lorde, Audre. "For Each of You." (1973) From a Land Where Ocher People Live. Broadside Press. Collected in Chosen Poems Old and New (1982) Norton.

85 Frankel, Todd, Shawn Boburg, Josh Dawsey, Ashley Parker, and Alex Horton. "The Gun That Divides a Nation." The Washington Post. March 27, 2023. And Guskin, Emily, Aadit Tambe and Jon Gerberg. "Why Do Americans Own AR-14S?" Washington Post. March 27, 2023.

86 Taylor, Sonya Renee. (2018) The Body is Not an Apology: The Power of Radical Self Love. Berrett – Koehler.

87 hooks, bell. "Toward a Worldwide Culture of Love". Lion's Roar: Buddhist Wisdom for Our Time. November 8, 2022.

88 brown, adrienne maree. 2009. "In Relationship with Others." adriennemareebrown.net. July 7, 2009.

ACKNOWLEDGEMENTS

First and importantly, my earnest thanks to Stewards of the Institute for Liberatory Innovation past and present: Sumeet Ajmani, Lyn Chamberlin, Anamari Gaeta, Melissa Gopnik, Erin Gravelle, Kris Hege, Robin Humell, Jordan Laney, and Chris Riddell. Each has made this book possible with their unique perspective, generosity, and skill. Their belief in the work of the ILI holds it up, and often holds me up too.

Thanks also to readers of *Intersections*, the ILI newsletter, who read these essays first. I'm honored and encouraged by their thoughtful attention, and I'll keep working to earn it.

Our work at the ILI rests on action, struggle, and rejoicing long before and all around us. I have many teachers I've never met (many appear in these pages) who are part of and driving an upswell of restorative, liberatory change. To that history, and to those teachers, I am grateful.

I can't think alone; conversations with far too many to list here are woven into everything I write. For these particular essays, though, I'm grateful for thinking with Danielle Boutet, Anna DiStefano, Ann Driscoll, Pamela Olufemi Kennebrew, Mike McRaith, Elizabeth Minnich, Karena Montag, Lynn Garthwaite Olsen, Daniel Sewell, Becky Sparks, Janet Thompson, and — very much not least — Shelley Vermilya.

To those who stepped up and in at the 12th hour — you know who you are — whew, thank you.

www.ingramcontent.com/pod-product-compliance
Lightning Source LLC
Chambersburg PA
CBHW032055040426
42335CB00037B/775